IMAGES
of America

SAN FRANCISCO'S
JAPANTOWN

The Japantown Task Force, Inc.

ARCADIA
PUBLISHING

Published by Arcadia Publishing
Charleston, South Carolina

Library of Congress Catalog Card Number: 2005929618

For all general information contact Arcadia Publishing at:
Telephone 843-853-2070
Fax 843-853-0044
E-mail sales@arcadiapublishing.com
For customer service and orders:
Toll-Free 1-888-313-2665

Visit us on the Internet at www.arcadiapublishing.com

The San Francisco Japanese Church of Christ's (now Christ United Presbyterian Church) Golden Jubilee was held in October 1936, at the Buchanan YMCA. The 50th anniversary celebrated the founding of the first Japanese Presbyterian church in America and honored the late Earnest A. Sturge, M.D., who played a major role in the establishment of the church in 1885 and the Japanese YMCA in 1886. (Courtesy of Christ United Presbyterian Church.)

CONTENTS

Acknowledgments   6

Introduction   7

1.   Birth of Nihonjin Machi   9

2.   A Thriving Community   39

3.   Families Uprooted by War Hysteria   55

4.   Starting Over Again . . . and Again   73

5.   Community Spirit and Celebration   91

6.   Preservation for the Generations   123

ACKNOWLEDGMENTS

This book was made possible by the guidance and participation of the Japantown Taskforce Book Review Committee: Hatsuro Aizawa; Seiko Fujimoto, Japanese Benevolent Society of California; Sumi Honnami; Greg Marutani, San Francisco Japanese American Citizens League; Karl Matsushita, Japanese American National Library (JANL); Judith Nihei; Katherine Reyes; Rosalyn Tonai, National Japanese American Historical Society (NJAHS); Himeo Tsumori; Bill Wong, editor and journalist; and Ken Yamada.

Special appreciation to Ben Pease, cartographer and research; Linda Jofuku, executive director, Japantown Taskforce, Inc.; John Poultney, editor, Arcadia Publishing; and the dedicated long hours of Darryl Abantao, JTF intern; Misako Mori, JTF intern; Lucy Kishiue, consultant and project manager, Clyde Izumi, technical support, San Francisco Foundation; Haas Jr. Fund; and Union Bank of California.

We especially extend our deepest appreciation to those who have shared their photographs and personal stories about San Francisco's Japantown: Ruth Asawa; Blue Collar Asian Women; Christ United Presbyterian Church; Cathy Inamasu, Nihonmachi Little Friends; consulate general of Japan, Honorable Makoto Yamanaka and consul Takashi Oda; Doug Dawkins and Tanako Hagiwara, Hagiwara family; Steve Doi, Nichi Bei Kai; Rev. Richard Grange, Japanese American Religious Federation and Konko-Kyo Church; Hamilton Senior Center; Richard Hashimoto and the Tak Matsuba-Japantown Merchants Association; James Hirabayashi; Ikenobo Ikebana Society of America; Doug Inouye, Boy Scout Troop No. 29; Japanese Community Youth Council (JCYC); Japantown Arts and Media; Kinmon Gakuen; Calvert Kitazumi; Dr. William Kiyasu; Kokoro Assisted Living; Janice Mirikitani, poet laureate; Albert Mizuhara; Arrice Mizono Mori; Sandy Mori, Kimochi; Morning Star School; May Murata, May's Cafe; Johnny Nagano; Nobiru-Kai; June-ko Nakagawa, San Francisco Radio Mainichi; Flo Nakamura; National Japanese American Citizens League (JACL); Nihonmachi Street Fair; Nikkei Lions Club; Nisei Fishing Club; Ayako Nishimoto, Girl Scouts Troop No. 37; Nunotani family; Keith Oka, Seizo Oka family; George Okada; Bobby and Ricky Okamura, Benkyodo; Takeshi Onishi, Japan Video and Media, Inc. and Issui-Kai; Bob Otsuka, California Flower Mart; Lois Ohwa, Togasaki family; Pine United Methodist Church; St. Xavier Church; Uoki Sakai family; Sakura Matsuri, Inc.; San Francisco Public Library, History Center; San Francisco Redevelopment Agency; Shinichi Seino, Kinokuniya Book Stores of America; Susan Snyder, Bancroft Library; Kenji Taguma, Nichi Bei Times; Isago Isao Tanaka; Ryuma and Grand Master Tanaka, San Francisco Taiko Dojo; Yukiko Tanaka, Boy Scout Troop No. 12; Rev. Kiko Tatedera, Soto Mission of San Francisco, Sokoji (Zen Temple); William Tsukamoto; Rev. Kodo Umezu, Buddhist Churches of American and the San Francisco Buddhist Church; Chiyo Wada; Rich Wada; Paul Osaki; Chris Hirano; Marjorie Fletcher; Ken Maeshiro, Japanese American History Archives (JAHA)/Japanese Community and Cultural Center of Northern California (JCCCNC); J. K. Yamamoto, Hokubei Mainichi; Joyce Yamamoto; and Jean Nakatani Yego.

INTRODUCTION

In 1853, Commo. Matthew Perry of the United States Navy and his fleet of gunships entered Tokyo harbor. Perry's arrival forced a reclusive nation to open trade with the United States and exposed the people of Japan to western ideas and culture.

The first Japanese immigrants sailed into San Francisco Bay in 1869, with hopes and dreams of a better life. This first generation, known as the *Issei,* was small in number and consisted mainly of young men. San Francisco was one of the primary ports of entry for early Japanese immigrants.

Western ideas gained interest and resulted in the early immigration of students with intentions to study in America and return to Japan. Around 1868, the attraction to America shifted from education to employment with the onset of a depression in Japan. These early immigrants had the intention to earn money and return to Japan but many settled to establish shops, hotels, restaurants, and rooming houses. From 1900 to 1909, Japanese businesses quickly grew from 90 to 545 establishments in San Francisco. They initially settled on the edge of the city's Chinatown, and in the working-class South of Market district, until the 1906 earthquake devastated these areas. The Japanese community relocated to the present Japantown area in the Western Addition, with another smaller concentration in South Park (south of Market, between Second and Third Streets and Brannan and Townsend).

As more immigrants arrived, social institutions arose to serve them. In 1877, the *Fukuin Kai* (Japanese Gospel Society) believed to be the first Japanese organization in the United States began meeting at the Chinese Methodist Mission in Chinatown. In the late 19th century, several more Japanese Christian organizations were established and spread to a growing number of other Japanese communities along the West Coast, through the central valley of California, to the Pacific Northwest, Midwest, South, and eventually the entire United States. By 1898, San Francisco was headquarters for Buddhist churches and social organizations located throughout the West, including prefectural associations or *kenjin-kai,* benevolent associations, and newspapers.

San Francisco's Japantown was originally known as *Nihonjin machi*—"Japanese people's town." It is the oldest of its kind in the continental United States and one of only three remaining Japantowns in the United States. Until 1906, San Francisco was the chief U.S. port of entry for Asian immigration with the largest *Nikkei* (Japanese) population of any mainland American city. Numerous social, economic, and political organizations originated in the city, including several churches such as the Buddhist Churches of America, the Japanese American Evangelical and Reform church, the Japanese Presbyterian Church, Konko-Kyo Church, the Japanese Young Women's Christian Association and Young Men's Christian Association, Pine Methodist Church, the Japanese Salvation Army, and civic organizations such as Japanese Benevolent Society, Japanese Association of American, and the Japanese American Citizens League.

By the turn of the 20th century, as the size of the community continued to increase, racist opposition to Japanese immigration began to coalesce, led by San Francisco mayor and later California Sen. James D. Phelan. Hostility worsened after the Japanese victory in the 1905 Russo-Japanese War raised fears of Japanese military power. However, much of the animosity was still couched in terms of economic rivalry between Japanese immigrants and surrounding communities.

San Francisco was a center of this antipathy. Following the 1906 earthquake, the San Francisco Board of Education adopted a policy intended, for the first time, to restrict Japanese American students to the segregated school previously established for Chinese American students. When the Japanese government protested, this local policy became an international dispute. Pres. Theodore Roosevelt intervened to urge that the policy be rescinded, and the school board agreed only in return for a promise by Roosevelt to stem Japanese immigration. In response, Roosevelt negotiated the 1908 "Gentlemen's Agreement" between the United States and Japan, by which further immigration of Japanese laborers was drastically reduced.

The Gentlemen's Agreement, however, did permit immigration of wives whose husbands were already living in the United States, including "picture brides," many who had never met their husbands prior to immigrating. Some 20,000 picture brides entered the U. S. from 1907 to 1924. Unlike the Chinese experience, immigration of Japanese women was an important step towards establishment of families and furtherance of the community. This provision marked an important shift in the nature of the Japanese community in San Francisco, by facilitating the establishment of families and of the second generation, the *Nisei*, who were citizens by birth and therefore legally able to own property. Institutions to serve the changing community quickly grew, including Japanese language schools and preschools for the rapidly Americanizing *Nisei*, as a means of preserving the community's Japanese culture. However, the Immigration Act of 1924 completely curtailed immigration from Japan until 1952.

Further undue hardship was imposed on Japanese immigrants such as the 1913 California law, in the form of the Heney-Webb Alien Land Act, that forbade property ownership by "aliens ineligible for citizenship" (at the time, immigrants from Asia were not permitted to become naturalized citizens). Given the population of California at the time, this restriction applied almost exclusively to Japanese immigrants and remained in effect until 1952. Antimiscegenation laws prohibiting interracial marriages prevailed until the 1960s.

The story of the Japanese Americans in San Francisco goes beyond the boundaries of *Nihonjin machi*. Some of these moments are captured in this book by way of photographs. The authors submit that this book cannot capture the complete history of San Francisco's Japantown. So much of the rich history lies with the families of the early *Issei* pioneers who bravely settled in a new world. This book is dedicated to these pioneers for their courage, sense of adventure, and their perseverance to succeed in building a new life.

One

BIRTH OF
NIHONJIN MACHI

The *Issei* (first-generation) pioneers settled in several areas of the city—many in Chinatown, along Dupont (later Grant) between California and Bush Streets. Others settled in South of Market, a neighborhood of working-class rooming houses, small businesses, and industries bounded by Market, Howard, Fifth, and Seventh Streets. Most Japanese establishments were on the back alleys, such as Stevenson and Jessie. Many young men lived outside these districts, working as domestic servants in middle- and upper-class houses in Nob Hill and Pacific Heights.

Both the South of Market and Chinatown areas were destroyed by the 1906 earthquake and fire. Emerging from the ashes, the Japanese community relocated in the city's Western Addition and South Park areas. A few businesses returned to Chinatown, lasting until World War II.

South Park was strategically located between the Southern Pacific Railroad station and the shipping docks used by Japanese shipping companies. This specialized district mainly served travelers to and from Japan, and to and from the western United States. By 1910, *Issei*-operated hotels and general stores were prominent on the north side of South Park Street. In 1924, these businesses suffered with the Immigration Act of 1924 blocking the flow of newcomers from Japan. In 1933, docks of cargo ships were moved north of the area to Piers 25 and 35.

Following the 1906 earthquake, San Francisco's Japanese relocated to the Western Addition in significant numbers. A new *Nihonjin machi* began to take hold primarily in the areas between Laguna and Webster, and Geary and Bush Streets.

The T. Z. Shiota Antique and Curios store located at 629 Dupont Street (Grant Avenue) was one of two stores Shiota owned in Chinatown, c. 1902. Chinatown was the major business district for early Japanese merchants. (Courtesy of JAHA/JCCCNC.)

These young men, gathered in 1898, are emblematic of a variety of Japanese social groups of this period. The YMCA, Japanese Methodist and Presbyterian churches, and Buddhist Mission provided places of worship and English classes for newcomers. Kenjin-kai clubs organized by people from particular *kens* (prefectures) were a place to celebrate regional customs and also served as credit unions and benevolent associations. (Courtesy of NJAHS, California Historical Society.)

The San Francisco Buddhist *Fujinkai* (Women's Auxiliary) was founded in 1900. Women took on many church responsibilities, including *toban* (care of the temple), hospital visits, church bazaars, raising funds for furnishings, the annual *Bon Odori* ceremonies, and hosting visitors. (Courtesy of Buddhist Churches of America.)

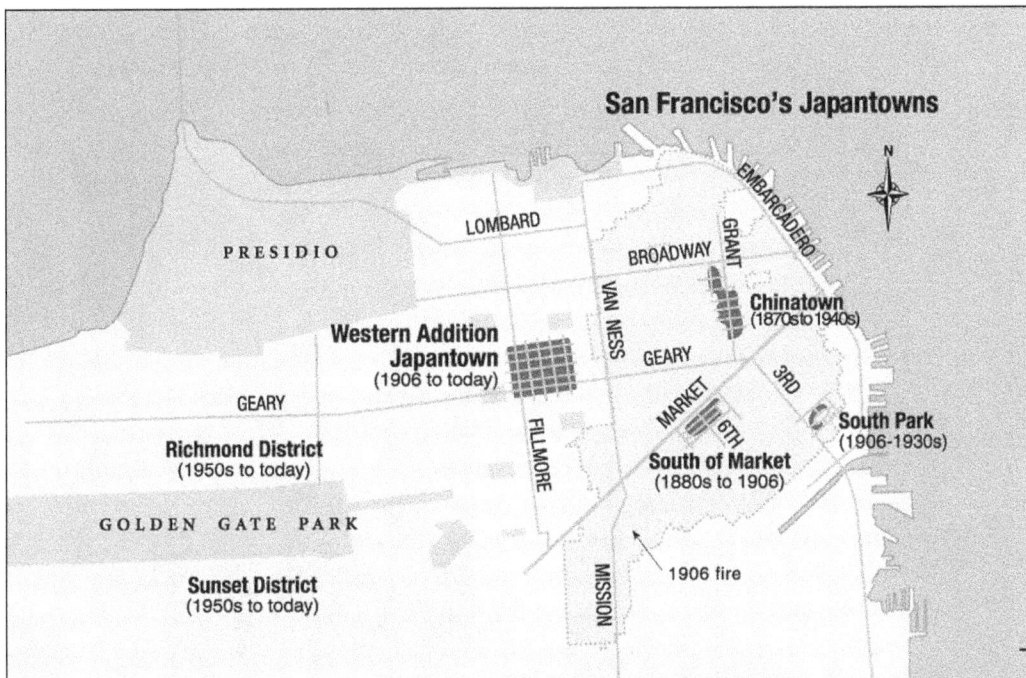

This map shows a chronology of San Francisco's *Nihonjin machis*. (Courtesy of Ben Pease.)

Matsunosuke Tsukamoto (standing, fourth from left) immigrated in 1887 to San Francisco, one of only 2,000 Japanese in America at that time. He established Sunset Laundry, the first Japanese-operated machine laundry in San Francisco in the late 1890s. Here he attends the Akitani wedding reception, *c.* 1905. (Courtesy of Will Tsukamoto.)

11

減軋裝置

明治三年七月廿二日

第七二〇號

水原兵助

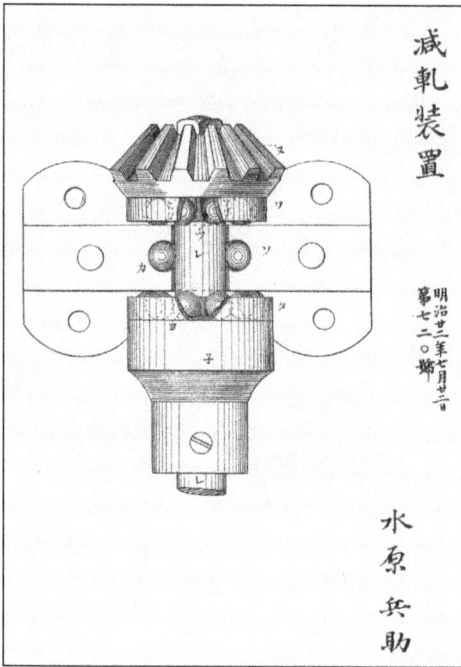

Hyosuke Mizuhara was trained in Scotland at a maritime academy and captained commercial ships in Japan. In 1893, he immigrated to America and found employment at Nathan Dohrmann Company, importer of Asian and European art goods, repairing art damaged in transit. Before his sudden departure from Japan in 1893, Mizuhara invented and received a Japanese patent for the ball bearing. (Courtesy of Albert Mizuhara.)

Sadataru Akiya (second from left) and others enjoy an outing in Stern Grove, c. 1906 (Courtesy of Joyce Yamamoto.)

In 1870, the first consulate for Japan in the United States was Charles Walcott Brooks, a U.S. national in San Francisco. San Francisco has played a significant role as a gateway throughout history of the American-Japanese relations. The first Japanese national to serve as consul, in 1876, was Kentaro Yanagiya. (Courtesy of Consulate of Japan.)

In October 1909, children, teachers, and families pose in the backyard of Nippon Gakuen Japanese Grammar School. Located at 1763 Sutter Street near Buchanan Street, this was one of several schools the *Issei* established to meet the needs of new families and teach children Japanese language and culture. (Courtesy of NJAHS.)

Hale's Department Store, on Market Street near Sixth Street, stands in ruins following the 1906 earthquake and fire. Many of the city's Japanese residents lived in the closely packed, wood-frame rooming houses south of Market between Fifth and Seventh Streets. In the fire's wake, only a forest of chimneys remained. (Courtesy of Hagiwara family collection.)

This view from lower Nob Hill overlooks Old St. Mary's Church (left), Chinatown, and the Financial District. On Dupont Street (Grant Avenue), in the foreground, had stood many Japanese-owned businesses, including art supply stores, restaurants, mercantile stores, a shooting

From Market and Larkin Streets, the Hagiwara family photographed the remains of the San Francisco City Hall, which stood just a few blocks from the South of Market Japantown, near today's United Nations Plaza. (Courtesy of Hagiwara family collection.)

gallery, and bookstores. Several Japanese families rebuilt and continued to do business on Grant Avenue until World War II; however, most relocated to the Western Addition. (Courtesy of Hagiwara family collection.)

In 1906, Suyeichi Okamura opened Benkyodo, one of the original businesses in Japantown. It is the last remaining manufacturer of *mochi* and *manju* in San Francisco. This photograph was taken in front of the store that was located on Geary Street. (Courtesy of Bobby and Ricky Okamura.)

Strategically located near the Embarcadero piers and Southern Pacific depot, South Park's small Japantown served Japanese travelers from 1906 to the 1930s. Pictured, from left to right, are Omiya Shoten souvenir shop, Omiya Hotel, Biwako Baths, and Hotel Bo-Chow Hotel (at corner). In the distance are the Kumamoto Hotel (fourth from corner) and the Eimoto Hotel (with curved facade). (Courtesy of JAHA/JCCCNC.)

Several families made a living in South Park by serving travelers on their way to and from Japan and inland parts of California. The four-story Hotel Bo-Chow was located at 102 South Park Street. (Courtesy of Hatsuro Aizawa.)

Japanese travelers, their families, and businessmen gathered at South Park every two weeks, anticipating the arrival of ships from Japan. At far right is the Omiya Hotel. Beneath the large sign, is Omiya Shoten souvenir shop and Biwako Baths. After Japanese businesses left in the 1930s, South Park went on to serve new working-class people, including Filipino and Latino immigrants, African Americans, and dot-com workers. (Courtesy of JAHA/JCCCNC.)

The Morino family operated the Omiya Hotel at 108 South Park Street. Pictured here on July 22, 1916, are Shokichi Morino (40 years old) with his daughter Chiyoko (three years) and son George (12 months). (Courtesy of JAHA/JCCCNC.)

The Miho family and friends pose in South Park where they operated the Higoya Hotel. Pictured here, from left to right, are (first row) unidentified, Yoneko Morino, Mary, Florence, Chizu, Rey, Kiki, and two unidentified people; (second row) Shikuzo Miho, Shime Miho, Jim Mitsuda, and Mrs. Yoneda. (Courtesy of Florence Nakamura.)

The Eimoto Hotel at 22 South Park was the first stop in the United States for many Japanese immigrants. Known today as the Madrid Hotel, it serves as a 45-unit residence for formerly homeless adults. (Courtesy of JAHA/JCCCNC.)

This *c.* 1907 group photograph shows the send-off of a friend traveling back to Japan by passenger ship. (Courtesy of Will Tsukamoto.)

The funeral for Minosabu Hayashi is seen here, *c.* 1910. (Courtesy of Will Tsukamoto.)

Troop No. 12 was the first Japanese American Boy Scout troop. Pictured here in 1915, from left to right, are (first row) Shizuo Ichikawa, Shin Shibata, Kanji Naritomi, and Tetsuya Ishimaru; (second row) Tom Murata, Masanobu Norisuye, Joe Sano, Yoshizo Sano, Edwin Katow, Susumu Togasaki, and Toru Hasegawa. (Courtesy of JAHA/JCCCNC.)

A family picnic takes place in the Sunset District around 1915. (Courtesy of Will Tsukamoto.)

By 1910, many Japanese businesses were located on Geary Street between Laguna and Buchanan Streets. Pictured here, from left to right, are Yabuno Brothers Grocery, Soto Ryokan (hotel), Nagasaki-ya Hotel (behind near wagon), Uoki K. Sakai fish store (left of second horse), Tanaka Shokai Grocery and Rice Mill, and Benkyo-do Bakery. Although these Victorians were built in the 1870s, most of the storefronts were added following the 1906 earthquake. (Courtesy of NJAHS.)

By 1925, Uoki K. Sakai moved one block north to 1684 Post Street near Buchanan Street. The Sakai family lived in the Victorian dwelling above their store. In addition to selling fish, the Sakais reprovisioned ships docking on the Embarcadero. (Courtesy of NJAHS.)

After losing their home in Chinatown in the 1906 earthquake, the Mizuhara family moved to 1823 Sutter Street. Mr. Mizuhara reopened their art repair shop with his sons Kikui and Katsui. Katsui Mizuhara is pictured here in his early 30s. The younger Mizuhara invented and received a U.S. patent on special cement used to repair porcelain, but it was deemed impractical for consumer use. (Courtesy of Albert Mizuhara.)

Around 1923, Kyutaro Abiko, publisher of the *Nichi Bei Shimbun* newspaper, throws the first pitch for the California Japanese American baseball tournament on St. Ignatius grounds at the University of San Francisco. (Courtesy of NJAHS.)

The San Francisco KDC baseball team was one of the first *Issei* teams around 1904. Baseball provided a common bond between the Japanese immigrant community and the white Western world, in hopes of improving communication and respect. (Courtesy of NJAHS/Frank Tsyaki family.)

A 1920s group photograph shows rival teams from Berkeley (B) and San Francisco (S) and are as follows: (first row) Kishi, Hada, Hauyashi, Fujita, and Yamasaki; (second row) Katagama, Fujii, two unidentified, and Nonaka; (third row) Takahashi, Takaishi, and Kiyasu. (Courtesy of Dr. William Kiyasu.)

The mission of the Presbyterian church was to teach Japanese immigrants good character and values, which they could take back to Japan for the advancement of the country. This 1910 Bible study group poses with Dr. Earnest Sturge (front row center), who played a major role in establishing the first Japanese Presbyterian church in the United States in 1885. In 1886, he also helped establish the Japanese YMCA. (Courtesy of Christ United Presbyterian Church.)

...Asiatics Must Not Be Naturalized...

NO JAPS IN OUR SCHOOLS

CITIZENS'

MASS MEETING

Will be held in

WALTON'S PAVILION

GOLDEN GATE AVENUE AND BUCHANAN STREET

Sunday Afternoon Dec. 23

AT 2 O'CLOCK

Under the Auspices of the

Japanese & Korean Exclusion League

O. A. TVEITMOE, Presiding Officer

The Meeting will be Addressed by

MAYOR EUGENE E. SCHMITZ

HON. FRANK McGOWAN,   W. R. HAGGERTY,
Attorney   President San Francisco Labor Council.
WALTER MACARTHUR,   P. H. McCARTHY,
Editor, Coast Seamen's Journal.   Pres. State & Local Bldg. Trades Councils.

AND OTHER PROMINENT CITIZENS

RAIN OR SHINE

Be Sure to Attend and Register Your Protest by Your Presence

In late 1906, the San Francisco Board of Education adopted a policy to restrict Japanese American students to the segregated school previously established for Chinese American students. At that time, the city had only 93 Japanese students. The *Issei*, unable to sway the school board or the governor, appealed to the Japanese consulate, who asked Pres. Theodore Roosevelt to intervene. (Courtesy of NJAHS.)

Teachers, students, and parents gather in front of Sano School, located in the backyard of 1761–1765 Sutter Street. The Sanos founded this school in 1906 as part of the *Issei* boycott of the San Francisco Board of Education's policy to segregate Japanese American students. Today this site is the national headquarters of the Japanese American Citizens League (JACL). (Courtesy of SF Redevelopment Agency/K. Hoshino collection.)

The Buddhist Church of San Francisco relocated to this Italianate dwelling at 1617 Gough Street following the 1906 earthquake, which destroyed the previous temple at 807 Polk Street. In 1910, the membership purchased property at 1881 Pine Street, one block west of this site, and built a new temple. It opened in 1914. (Courtesy of Buddhist Churches of America.)

A group poses in front of the Japanese Pavilion at the 1915 Panama-Pacific International Exposition. The exposition was a nine-month celebration commemorating the completion of the Panama Canal, the reconstruction of San Francisco, and the 400th anniversary of Spanish explorer Vasco Nunez de Balboa's discovery of the Pacific Ocean. (Courtesy of JANL.)

Although they were not U.S. citizens, some *Issei* volunteered for the U.S. armed forces in World War I. In 1918, these young men gather for a send-off celebration for U.S. Army enlistee Keitaro Tsukamoto at 1619 Laguna Street, home of the Japanese Association (Soko Club). (Courtesy of JAHA/JCCCNC.)

Kitsuda and Kunisada Kiyasu enlisted in the U.S. Army during World War I. Here they pose in uniform on the campus of the University of California, Berkeley, c. 1918. Both men went on to serve as doctors for many years in San Francisco's Japantown. (Courtesy of Dr. William Kiyasu.)

Keitaro Tsukamoto (seated center) joined the U. S. Army and was sent to France and Belgium around 1918. Here soldiers are practicing Morse code in their barracks. (Courtesy of Will Tsukamoto.)

The 1919 San Francisco *Nihonjin-kai* welcome-back celebration of World War I enlistees is seen here. (Courtesy of Will Tsukamoto.)

Makoto Hagiwara, right, immigrated in 1886. He opened the first Japanese restaurant in San Francisco, and is credited with inventing the fortune cookie. In 1894, Makoto was hired as curator of the Japanese Tea Garden. In 1925, Goro Hagiwara, center, took over management following Makoto's death. In 1937, George Hagiwara, left, assisted in the management of the tea garden upon Goro's death. (Courtesy of Hagiwara family collection.)

Japanese Tea Garden grounds, with many of the original structures and plantings installed and tended by the Hagiwara family, may still be found today. (Courtesy of Hagiwara family collection.)

The original teahouse from the 1894 Midwinter Exposition is seen in this 1900 photograph, taken prior to the Hagiwara eviction. The teahouse features traditional designs and bronze cranes in the garden area. (Courtesy of Hagiwara family collection.)

An automobile at the gate to the Japanese Tea Garden. It was common to greet dignitaries and guests at this entrance. The gate is no longer in use, but was restored by traditional craftsmen and still stands today. (Courtesy of Hagiwara family collection.)

In 1900, the Hagiwara family established the Japanese Village at 178 H Street (now Lincoln Way) after the city took management of the tea garden away from Makoto Hagiwara because of racial prejudice. The tea garden fell into such disrepair that, in 1907, the city asked Makoto to return and lease it as a concession for $1 a year. (Courtesy of Hagiwara family collection.)

Kikunatsu and Shigeko (Kushida) Togasaki's silver anniversary photograph, c. 1920. He journeyed to America while waiting to be appointed to a judgeship in Japan. His wife came to the United States on a Woman's Christian Union scholarship. Both were strong-willed pioneers and few thought the marriage would last. (Courtesy of Lois Ohwa.)

This c. 1920 family portrait shows the Togasaki's with their children—George Kiyoshi, Susumu, Kazue, Teru, Yoshiye, Yaye, Mitsuye, and Chiye. In the early 1880s, the family immigrated from Japan, and was a beacon for the community with three children becoming nurses and three becoming medical doctors. Their son George was part of the San Francisco school segregation incident. (Courtesy of Lois Ohwa.)

Hana Ohama was one of the many women who arrived in the United States through Angel Island Immigration Station. Pictured in 1912, she is dressed in the finest Western fashions. (Courtesy of NJAHS/George Ohama.)

In 1920, "picture brides" arrived at Angel Island. Arranged marriages were common in Japan and some 20,000 women entered the United States from 1907 to 1924. The passage of the Immigration Act of 1924 completely curtailed immigration from Japan until 1952. (Courtesy of NJAHS.)

San Francisco's *Shin Sekai (New World)* Japanese newspaper set up a table on Post Street in Japantown to collect relief funds for Tokyo's great earthquake and fire in 1923. (Courtesy of JAHA/JCCCNC.)

The Kashu Hotel, operated by Sakutaro Nakano in 1927, was located on Laguna and Sutter Streets and was a center of social activities in its heyday. The owner was Sakanosuke Imura of Alameda, whose son Haruo took over after World War II. Known as the Kirkland Hotel in the 1960s, it became dilapidated and was demolished in 1967. In 1975, it became the site of Christ United Presbyterian Church. (Courtesy of JAHA/JCCCNC.)

In 1901, pioneers of the community built the Japanese Cemetery in Colma City with a generous grant from the Emperor Meiji of Japan. The Japanese Benevolent Society (*Kashu Nikkeijin Jikeikai*) provides assistance to members of the community and maintains relations between the Japanese government and the *Nikkei* community. In June 1922, a group gathers to commemorate the society's 20th anniversary. (Courtesy of San Francisco Public Library, History Center.)

In the late 1880s, a group of San Francisco Japanese associations gathered to address the community's need for a Japanese educational system, motivated largely by an 1895 school exclusion law passed by the San Francisco Board of Education. In 1911, the *Kinmon Gakuen* (Golden Gate School) opened. This group gathers on may 20, 1925, to celebrate *Kinmon Gakuen's* 17-year anniversary. (Courtesy of JANL.)

Pictured is the October 30, 1921, dinner that the "Potato King," George Shima, threw for Viscount Shibusawa of Japan at the Fairmont Hotel. (Courtesy of Will Tsukamoto.)

Around 1923, Suwa (Nakai) Honnami, standing, and Natsuko (Takagi) Nakatani worked together at Pacific Trading Company. (Courtesy of Jean Nakatani Yego.)

Employees of the Pacific Trading Company pose, c. 1923, outside their building on the Embarcadero waterfront. Founded in 1906 by Gunzo Sugihara and Kichitaro Niino, it was one of the largest import/export companies of food products to Japan. (Courtesy of Jean Nakatani Yego.)

Two

A Thriving Community

By the time of the 1910 census, the core area near Post and Buchanan Streets was home to more than 50 Japanese-owned commercial establishments, and to most of the 4,700 Japanese residents residing in the city. The community prospered through the 1920s and 1930s. By 1940, the Japanese population of Japantown, although by then second in size to Little Tokyo in Los Angeles, numbered over 5,000, with more than 200 Japanese-owned businesses. Long-established *Issei*-owned businesses were joined by emerging *Nisei* entrepreneurs.

Gosha-do Books and Stationery was located at 1698 Post Street. In this 1928 view, Kanemitsu Aizawa stands amidst floor-to-ceiling bookshelves and glass display cases with stationery and other supplies (note the stereo picture viewers at center). After World War II, this store became Soko Hardware, which remains today. Gosha-do reopened at 1705 Post Street until 1959. (Courtesy of Hatsuro Aizawa.)

Mrs. Misawa and Dr. Kiyasu are pictured here in the 1920s. Misawa Drug Store, located at 1602 Post Street, was the first registered Japanese pharmacy in San Francisco. (Courtesy of Dr. William Kiyasu.)

On April 5, 1929, a group of West Coast *Nisei* leaders gathered in San Francisco to plan a national organization. The Japanese American Citizens League (JACL) is one of the foremost champions in the cause of civil rights. (Courtesy of JANL/Mrs. Saburo Kido.)

Hatsuro (Hats) Aizawa, seen here in August 1924, became a successful businessman and community leader. (Courtesy of Aizawa family.)

The Japanese YMCA, founded in 1886 by Dr. Earnest Sturge, holds a bazaar in March 1930. (Courtesy of NJAHS/Tom Kawaguchi family.)

Members of the Evangelical and Reformed Church picnic and play in the sand dunes of the Sunset District, c. 1938. (Courtesy of Hatsuro Aizawa.)

This 1934 group photograph of Japantown journalists includes Michi (Oka) Onuma (front row, center), the first Japanese American female to be English editor of the *Nichi Bei Times* and the *Hokubei Mainichi*. A lifelong journalist, she worked on the newspaper *Heart Mountain Sentinel* (Wyoming) while interned in a World War II concentration camp. (Courtesy of Joyce Yamamoto.)

Archers compete with traditional long bows in the Hagiwara Japanese Tea Gardens, *c.* 1930 (Courtesy of Hagiwara family collection.)

The Japanese Archery Club gathers for a group photograph in 1930 at the Japanese Tea Garden, where they conducted target practice. (Courtesy of Hagiwara family collection.)

會奏獨カニモーハ迎歡氏男吉田友
援助ドンバカニモーハ港桑
日十三月五年九和昭

Morning Star School was a place of musical interests for everything from traditional Japanese folk songs to Western classical, jazz, and big band music. Pictured is the Harmonica Band. (Courtesy of NJAHS/Tom Kawaguchi family.)

惠喜眞彌阿本催主
會習温季春
日八月三年一十和昭
ルーホ星曉祭

The Honnami family actively participated in a 1936 koto recital: Taeko and Etsuko (first row, second and third; Sumi and Suwa "Makie" (second row, fourth and fifth); and Hikoroku (fourth row, third). (Courtesy of Sumi Honnami.)

Sumi (Hagiwara) Nagata and Namiko Hagiwara are in the Japanese Tea Garden around 1937. (Courtesy of Hagiwara family collection.)

The Hagiwara family, pictured here, from left to right, c. 1936, are Shigeo, Sumi, Haruko, Takano, Tai, Goro, and George. (Courtesy of Hagiwara family collection.)

The students in this 1933 class photograph reflect the diversity of the neighborhood. Rafael Weill Elementary School was located on the south edge of Japantown on Ellis Street near Webster Street. The school, named for a prominent Jewish merchant and civic leader, is now Rosa Parks Middle School. (Courtesy of Hatsuro Aizawa.)

Young musicians of the Japanese Association Marching Band pose on Buchanan Street near Sutter Street, c. 1935. Note the temporary bandstand decorated with cherry blossoms at right. Today this location is Buchanan Mall. The apartment building at left was replaced by the Miyako Inn. (Courtesy of JANL.)

Aoki Taisedo bookstore moved from Chinatown to 1601 Geary Street after the 1906 earthquake. In 1930, a new, larger store at 1656 Post Street held its grand opening. Aoki Taisedo was the largest bookstore in Japantown and also sold school supplies and Japanese phonograph records. Standing amidst the plants and banners, from left to right, are three unidentified, Hikoroku Honnami, owner Michitsugu Aoki, and Mr. Nishikawa. (Courtesy of Sumi Honnami.)

Mr. Inouye and employees pose in front of the Geary Street Cleaners (1938–1939). This business was one of half a dozen Japanese American cleaners in the neighborhood just prior to World War II. (Courtesy of Dr. Himeo Tsumori.)

In April 1939, girls in kimonos parade at the Golden Gate International Exposition on Treasure Island. As clouds of war gathered in the Pacific, San Francisco's Japanese American community participated proudly in the fair. Japan also participated by hosting a large pavilion at the exposition.

On April 29, 1939, the Japanese American community constructed this float for Japan Day at the Golden Gate International Exposition.

St. Francis Xavier Japanese Catholic Mission hold its 1936 confirmation with the archbishop of San Francisco (center). He is surrounded by Pastors William Stoecke and John Zimmerman and German priests from the Society of the Divine Word. (Courtesy of Sumi Honnami.)

In April 1936, members of the Japanese Methodist Episcopal Church gather to celebrate Easter Sunday. One of the first Japanese American Protestant churches, it has its roots in the Japanese Gospel Society of 1877. Now known as Pine United Methodist Church, it is located at 426 Thirty-third Avenue in the Richmond District. From 1894 to 1965, they worshipped at 1359 Pine Street. (Courtesy of NJAHS.)

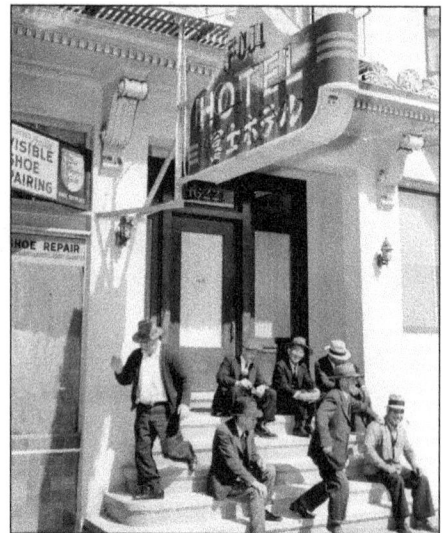

In April 1942, Mr. Tatsuno, above left, is pictured in his Nichibei Bussan department store at 1701 Post Street, prior to the evacuation/internment. Tatsuno was in the goods business for 40 years in San Francisco. Nichibei Bussan was able to reopen after World War II, and continued to sell goods under Tatsuno's son David, until his death in the mid 1980s. Above right, Japanese American men gather on the steps of the Fuji Hotel in the days between Pearl Harbor and the internment. The Fuji Hotel was at 1622-1632 Post Street (east side of today's Peace Plaza) and catered to day laborers and domestic workers, many of them bachelors. (Courtesy of Bancroft Library.)

The Muratas established Nippon Goldfish, located at 1919 Bush Street. This *c.* 1935 photograph shows ponds in which goldfish were raised; glass houses protected some fish against the weather. Nippon Goldfish shipped fish to customers in sealed cans via railway express; they employed two blacksmiths to fabricate custom aquariums. The Muratas returned after World War II, but were displaced to the Richmond District during the mid-1960s redevelopment. The store closed in 2005. (Courtesy of JAHA/JCCCNC.)

Jimmie Akiya is pictured in his ROTC uniform around 1941. His sister, Tomi (Akiya) Andow poses for this 1937 photograph at right. (Courtesy of Joyce Yamamoto.)

In April 1934, children and parents fill the sidewalk in front of the First Reformed Church (later the First Evangelical and Reformed Church) on Easter Sunday. Founded in 1910, the First Reformed Church moved into this old Victorian church at 1760 Post Street in 1913. Though bigger than their needs, the sanctuary easily accommodated the growing congregation, and the wider community used it for large meetings and ceremonies. (Courtesy of Hatsuro Aizawa.)

Initiated by the Japanese American, the California Flower Mart was established in 1909 and was the first grower-operated wholesale flower market on the Pacific Coast. The first site was located in an alley between Kearney and Montgomery Streets and Sutter and Post Streets. Pictured here around 1940 is a subsequent location on Market Street at Fifth and Howard Streets. (Courtesy of San Francisco Flower Mart/Bob Ostuka.)

CALIFORNIA FLOWER MARKET
Incorporated
October - 1940

The First Evangelical and Reformed Church celebrated its 31st anniversary on November 1941, just weeks before Pearl Harbor. During the internment, the building was home to several newly formed African American churches, including Macedonia Missionary Baptist Church. (Courtesy of Dr. Himeo Tsumori.)

This 1940 map shows Japantown and its businesses. (Courtesy of Ben Pease.)

Three

FAMILIES UPROOTED BY WAR HYSTERIA

The attack on Pearl Harbor in December 1941 by the Japanese Navy, abruptly ended the prosperity established by Japanese immigrants. In Japantown, prominent businessmen, clergy, and schoolteachers, tagged as "enemy aliens" and "trouble-makers," were rounded up by the FBI and separated from their families.

Anti-Japanese hysteria in San Francisco intensified as America entered World War II. In February 1942, Pres. Franklin D. Roosevelt signed Executive Order 9066, and by late March 1942, Gen. John L. DeWitt began issuing civilian exclusion orders, expelling "all persons of Japanese ancestry, including aliens and non-aliens" from West Coast military zones. In a little over four months, more than 120,000 Americans of Japanese ancestry were forced from their homes to internment camps under the guise of national security.

The entire Japanese community of San Francisco, both citizens and foreign-born, was ordered to register and eventually report for processing to various sites throughout San Francisco, including *Kinmon Gakuen*, the Japanese language school building on Bush Street, and the YMCA building on Buchanan Street. By April, they were sent to various "assembly centers"—primarily Tanforan in San Bruno, a racetrack hastily converted into a temporary detention camp—before being shipped out to one of 10 concentration camps located away from the West Coast. Residents from the San Francisco Bay Area were primarily placed in Topaz, near the town of Delta, in the Utah desert. Without charges, hearings, or trials, many families languished behind barbed wire until 1945.

A 1942 view of business district on Post Street. (Courtesy of Bancroft Library.)

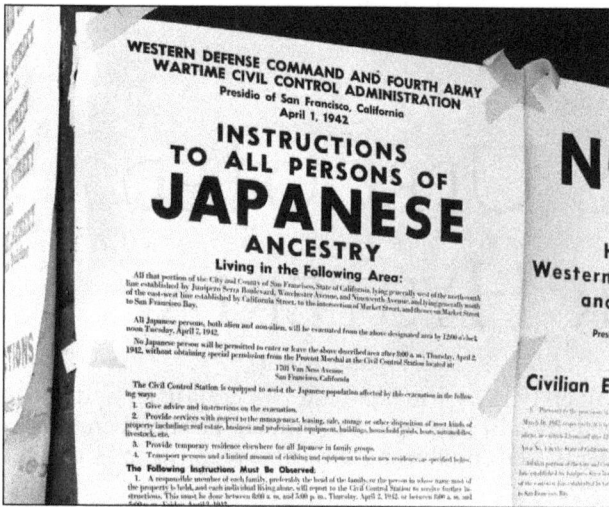

This exclusion order, posted at First and Front Streets, directs that "all Japanese persons, both alien and non-alien, will be evacuated." (Courtesy of Bancroft Library.)

On April 20, 1942, at Raphael Weill Public School, on Geary and Buchanan Streets, young Americans salute the flag on the playground. (Courtesy of Bancroft Library.)

On April 4, 1942, a closeout sale was held prior to evacuation at a store on Grant Avenue in Chinatown. It was operated by a proprietor of Japanese ancestry. (Courtesy of Bancroft Library.)

Nisei Grill, named after second-generation children born in this country to Japanese immigrants, was closed prior to eviction on April 19, 1942. According to the sign in the window, it was scheduled to reopen under new management on April 7, 1942. (Courtesy of Bancroft Library.)

Dave Tatsuno posts an evacuation sale sign in front of his Nichibei Bussan department store. Many residents and business had only days to sell and pack their belongings in April 1942. (Courtesy of NJAHS.)

On March 29, 1942, evidence of the forthcoming evacuation of residents of Japanese ancestry is seen in Japantown. (Courtesy of Bancroft Library.)

This March 1942 farewell letter was posted in the store window of T. Z. Shiota, an importer in San Francisco's Chinatown, after serving the public for 43 years. (Courtesy of Bancroft Library.)

On April 7, 1942, Post Street business owners board the windows of their stores prior to evacuation. (Courtesy of Bancroft Library.)

On April 25, 1942, people line up outside the Kimon Gakun auditorium at 2031 Bush Street to register for evacuation. (Courtesy of Bancroft Library.)

As a safeguard for health, evacuees were inoculated as they registered for evacuation at 2031 Bush Street. Nurses and doctors of Japanese ancestry administered the inoculations. (Courtesy of Bancroft Library.)

Residents wearing tags line up at the Japanese Buchanan YMCA, awaiting incarceration at Tanforan Racetrack in San Bruno while the 10 internment camps were being built. Two-thirds of internees were U.S. citizens.

The family unit was kept intact in various phases of evacuation. On April 6, 1942, the Wartime Civil Control Administration station, located at 2020 Van Ness Avenue, was the first group of 664 to be evacuated from San Francisco. (Courtesy of Bancroft Library.)

With all their possessions packed, two friends play a final game while awaiting evacuation on April 25, 1942. People were only allowed to take whatever they can carry. (Courtesy of Bancroft Library.)

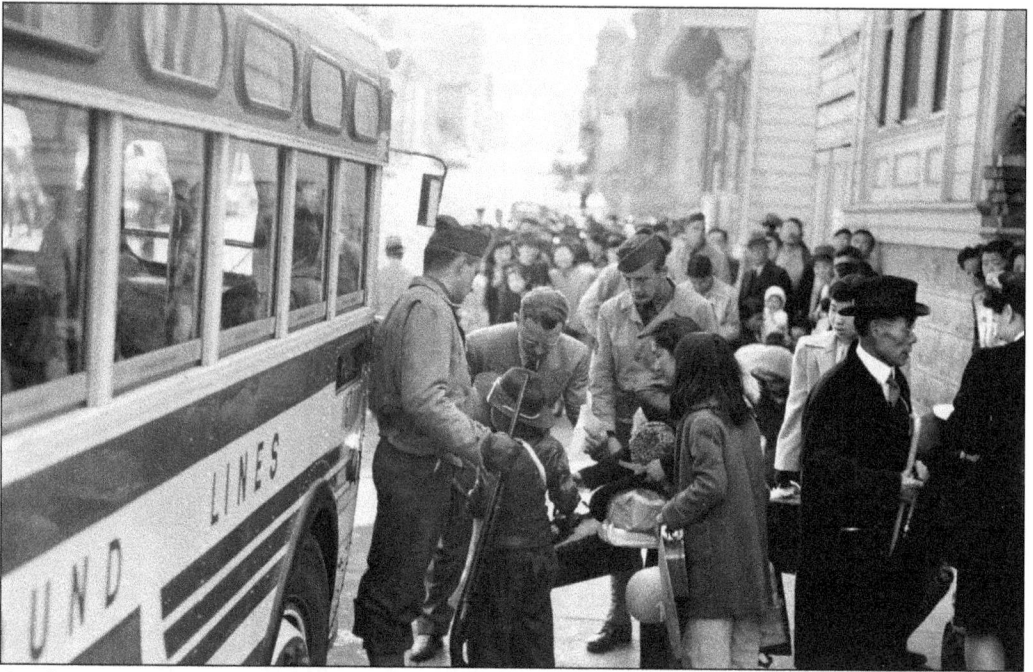

On the morning of April 29, 1942, about 660 merchants, shopkeepers, tradespeople, and professional people left their homes and were transported to Tanforan Assembly Center. This photograph shows a family about to get on the bus. The little boy in the new cowboy hat is having his identification tag checked by an official before boarding. (Courtesy of Bancroft Library.)

Inhabitants of Japantown wave farewell at the departure of their friends and neighbors, whom they will soon join at Tanforan Assembly Center. In three days, the streets of Japantown will be deserted. (Courtesy of Bancroft Library.)

Above left, a young boy, perhaps too young to understand, looks out the window of the bus that will take him to Tanforan Assembly Center in April 1942. At right, stripped of their belongings to only what they can carry, evacuees arrive at 2020 Van Ness Avenue. They wait to be transported and are unsure of what the future will be for them and their families. (Courtesy of Bancroft Library.)

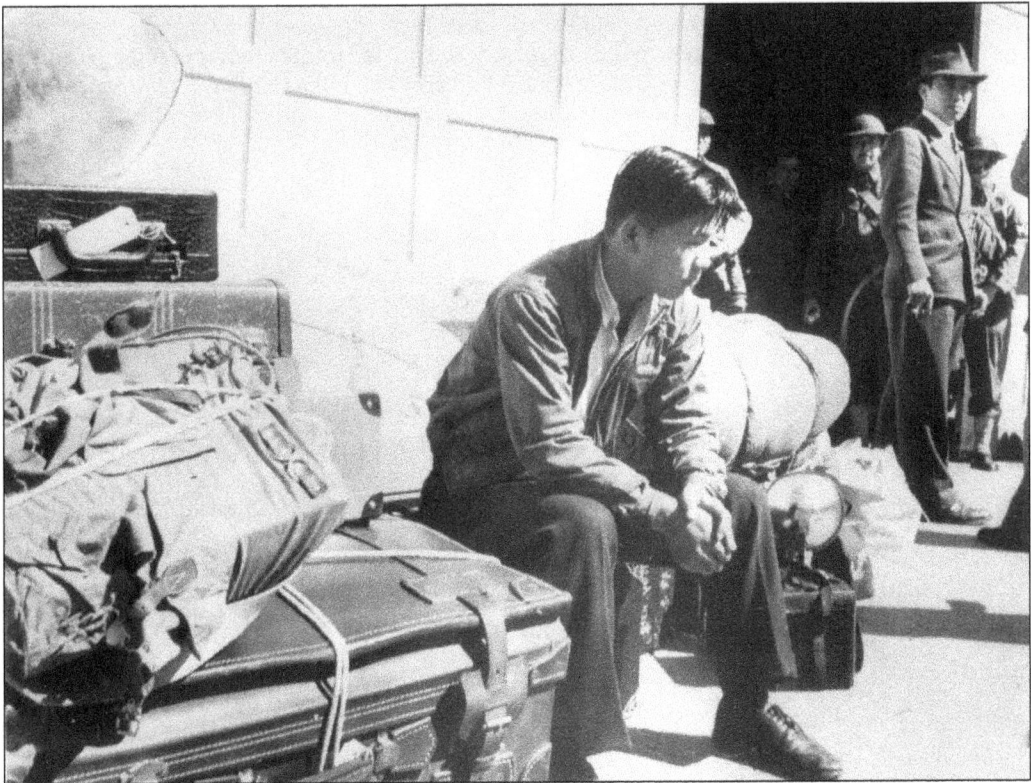

In April 1942, Mits Kojimoto waits with his belongings at 2020 Van Ness Avenue. (Courtesy of NJAHS.)

Bus-load after bus-load of evacuated people arrived at Tanforan Assembly Center. After going through the necessary procedure of registration, they are guided to the quarters assigned to them in the barracks. Evacuees lineup outside the mess hall at noon. Note the newly built barracks in the background in which family units are housed. (Courtesy of Bancroft Library.)

On September 15, 1942, the first internees arrive at the Topaz Concentration Camp greeted by wind, heat, and dust.

On October 3, 1944, students and teachers pose for a class photograph in Topaz, Utah. Two Hagiwara family members are pictured here—Tanako Hagiwara, front row, fourth from left, and Namiko Hagiwara, back row, far right. (Courtesy of Hagiwara family collection.)

Internees tried to cope with life in a concentration camp. Many planted vegetables and flowers if the conditions were suitable. This housing barrack was in Jerome, Arkansas. (Courtesy of Nunotani family.)

The Military Intelligence Service Language School opened at the Presidio of San Francisco on November 1, 1941. The instructors posing for a photograph near Crissy Field, from left to right, are Tom Tanimoto, Tets Imagawa, John Aiso, Aki Oshida, Shig Kihara, Tosh Tsukahira, Paul Tekawa, and Tad Yamada. (Courtesy of NJAHS/Gene Uratsu.)

In January 1942, *Nisei* soldiers of the Military Intelligence Service are at their lessons in the former airmail hangar at Crissy Field. (Courtesy of NJAHS.)

Wally Nunotani, in combat uniform, served in the 442nd Regimental Combat Team in I Company. (Courtesy of Nunotani family.)

On October 14, 1944, Japanese American troops of the 2nd Battalion, 442nd Regimental Combat Team, Chambois sector, France, climb into a truck as they prepare to move to their bivouac area. (Courtesy of NJAHS.)

Via radio, military intelligence serviceman Karl Yoneda advises Japanese soldiers in the Pacific to surrender. (Courtesy of NJAHS.)

On October 14, 1944, Japanese American infantrymen in the 2nd Battalion, 442nd Regimental Combat Team, Chambois sector, France, hike up a muddy French road to their new bivouac area. (Courtesy of NJAHS.)

Gov. John Connally of Texas proclaimed the *Nisei* soldiers "Honorary Texans" in appreciation of their heroic rescue of the "Lost Battalion" of Texas in October 1944. This October 14, 1944, U.S. Army Signal Corps photograph, shows Company F of the 2nd Battalion, 442nd Regimental Combat Team, Chambois sector, France. (Courtesy of NJAHS.)

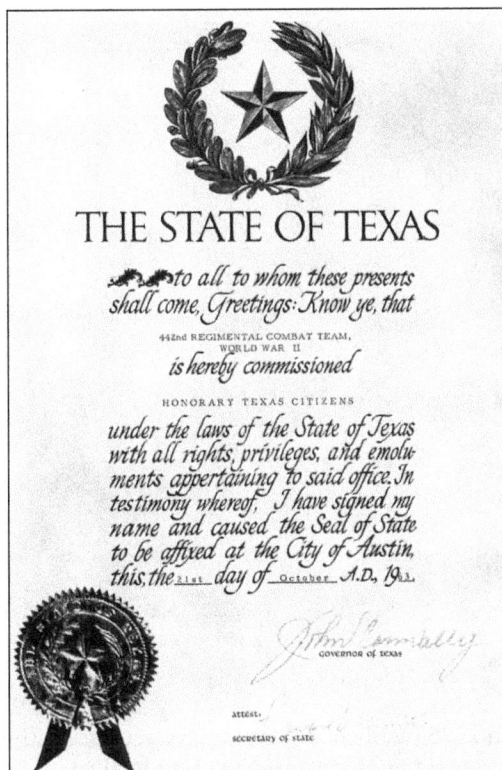

THE STATE OF TEXAS

to all to whom these presents shall come, Greetings: Know ye, that

442nd REGIMENTAL COMBAT TEAM, WORLD WAR II

is hereby commissioned

HONORARY TEXAS CITIZENS

under the laws of the State of Texas with all rights, privileges, and emoluments appertaining to said office. In testimony whereof, I have signed my name and caused the Seal of State to be affixed at the City of Austin, this the 21st day of October A.D. 1963.

GOVERNOR OF TEXAS

attest:

SECRETARY OF STATE

In October 1963, the "Honorary Texan" certificate was commissioned by Governor Connally. The 100th Infantry Battalion and the 442nd Regimental Combat Team, the most decorated unit in World War II, suffered over 800 casualties rescuing 211 men of the Texas "Lost Battalion" in October 1944 in Bruyeres, France. (Courtesy of Nunotani family.)

Members of the VFW Golden Gate Nisei Memorial Post No. 9879 conduct annual Memorial Day observances at the Golden Gate National Cemetery honoring fallen comrades. (Courtesy of Nunotani family.)

In 1998, Wally Nunotani, center, reunites with friends from the Battle of Bruyeres at the Legion of Honor. (Courtesy of Nunotani family.)

The Redress Movement began with the 1978 JACL national convention. Congress and the American public knew very little about the internment of Japanese Americans during World War II and education was critical for any legislative passage. In 1981, the Commission on Wartime Relocation and Internment of Civilians (CWRIC) held hearings at Golden Gate University, San Francisco. (Courtesy of Isao Isago Tanaka/NJAHS.)

The Civil Liberties Act of 1988, signed on August 10 by Pres. Ronald Reagan, extended a formal apology for the unjust incarceration of those surviving people impacted by Executive Order 9066. In 1990, one of the first redress checks, in the amount $20,000, was presented to Mitsu Sato at the Hinode Towers. (Courtesy of Rick Rocamora/NJAHS.)

In 1983, *coram nobis* team lawyers Dale Minami and Don Tamaki, along with researcher Peter Irons (seated), and Fred Korematsu, Gordon Hirabayashi, and Min Yasui (standing), meet the press at the Press Club of San Francisco. A team of young *Sansei* lawyers had begun the task of trying to get the convictions of Korematsu, Hirabayashi, and Yasui, men of Japanese ancestry who ignored internment orders, overturned. All three convictions were set aside, not overturned, in the U.S. district courts. The government chose not to appeal. (Courtesy of NJAHS/Chris Huie.)

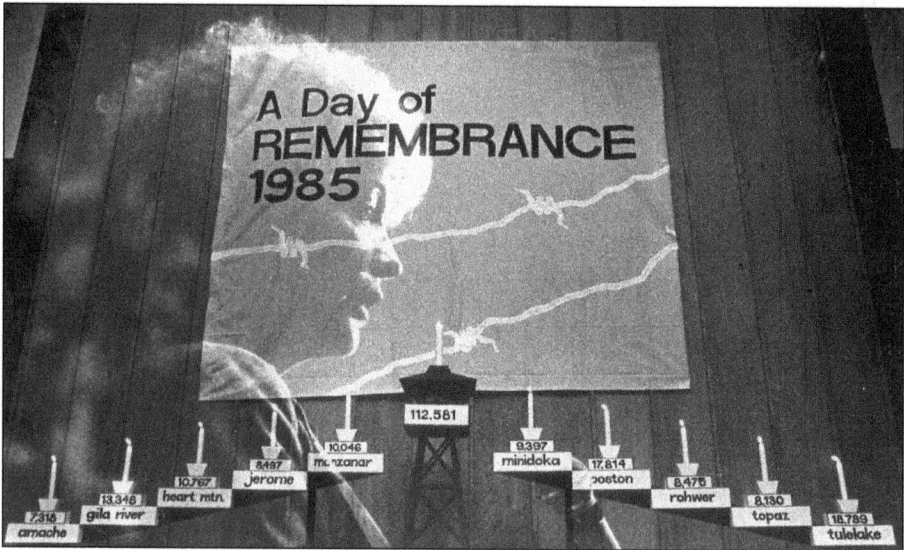

The annual Day of Remembrance, observed every February, commemorates Pres. Roosevelt's Executive Order 9066 that resulted in the incarceration of over 120,000 people of Japanese ancestry into internment camps from 1942–1945. For the observance in 1985, Chief Justice Rose Bird of California was the keynote speaker. (Courtesy of Isao Isago Tanaka/NJAHS.)

Four

STARTING OVER
AGAIN . . . AND AGAIN

Following the war, many Japanese Americans returned to San Francisco, now largely occupied by wartime defense industry workers. Starting over was a particular hardship for most Japanese American families returning from the camps. Temporary housing – sometimes in church social halls or former military housing – was often full. Reentry into society, from finding work to attending school, was often met with hostility and mistrust. By the 1950 census, although Japanese numbers in Japantown area were nearly back to their prewar levels, both whites and African Americans far outnumbered them. Japanese property ownership initially rebounded following the war. By 1950, 148 parcels were Japanese owned. This number rose to 186 by 1962, the end of the initial round of urban renewal condemnations.

In 1948, 27 blocks of San Francisco's Western Addition, including much of Japantown, was selected as one of the first large-scale urban renewal projects in the nation. This involved the mass clearance of the neighborhood through the use of eminent domain, including a large number of residences and small businesses. In order to address the "urban blight," the San Francisco Redevelopment Agency (SFRA) began acquiring properties in the late 1950s. This undertaking was conducted in two project areas, A-1 (south of Post Street) and A-2 (north of Post Street). The A-2, begun in 1966, had more community involvement. SFRA mandated "improvements," but allowed the Japanese American community to hire their own architects and planners to reshape the area between Post and Bush Streets—four blocks of the larger 43-block project.

In June 1945, Koutei Sugaya, returned from Topaz, Utah, to find everything in good condition. He reopened the Pine Street Laundry Company located at 2325 Pine Street near Fillmore Street. (Courtesy of Bancroft Library.)

Hatsuto Yamada had been a partner in the Nippon Drug Store before World War II. Returning from Topaz, he opened Jim's Drug Company at 1698 Sutter Street. In addition to serving his Japanese American neighbors, he exported drugs to war-torn Japan in the years following World War II, as drugs were in short supply. (Courtesy of Bancroft Library.)

In June 1945, Mr. and Mrs. Shotsu Gishifu and their son Kaoro stand in front of their cleaners at 1704 Laguna Street. (Courtesy of Bancroft Library.)

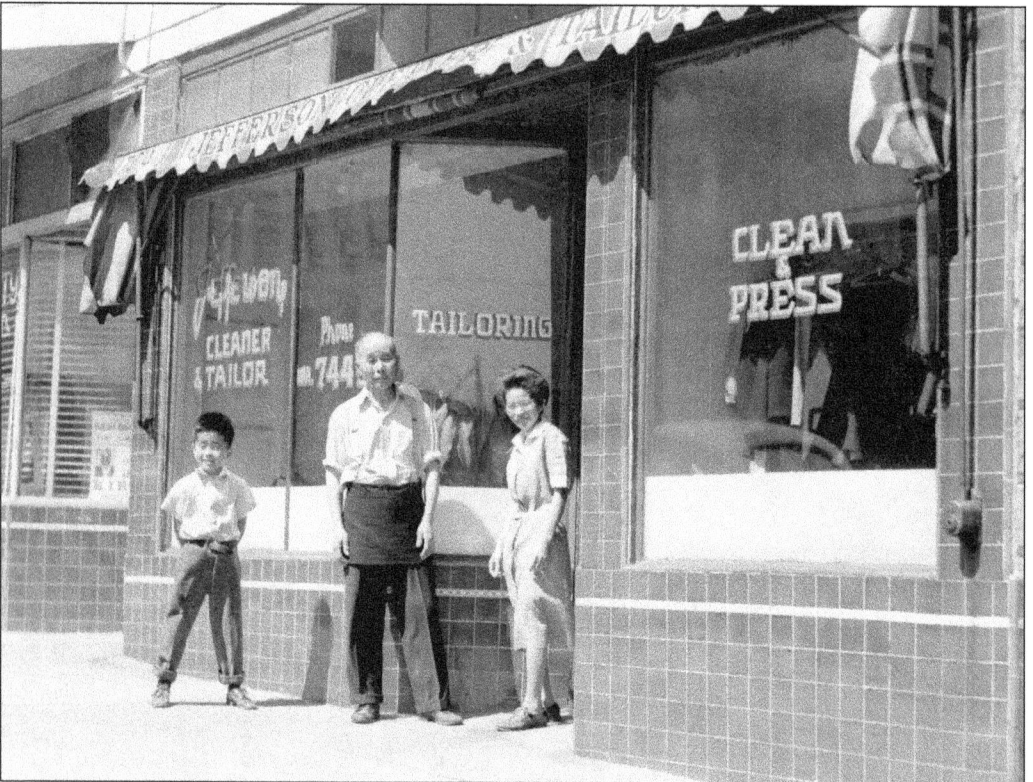

The Aki Hotel was one of several hotels in Japantown before and after World War II. Run by Mr. and Mrs. Ichiro Kataoka until 1959, it was torn down and replaced by the Miyako Hotel. (Courtesy of JAHA/JCCCNC.)

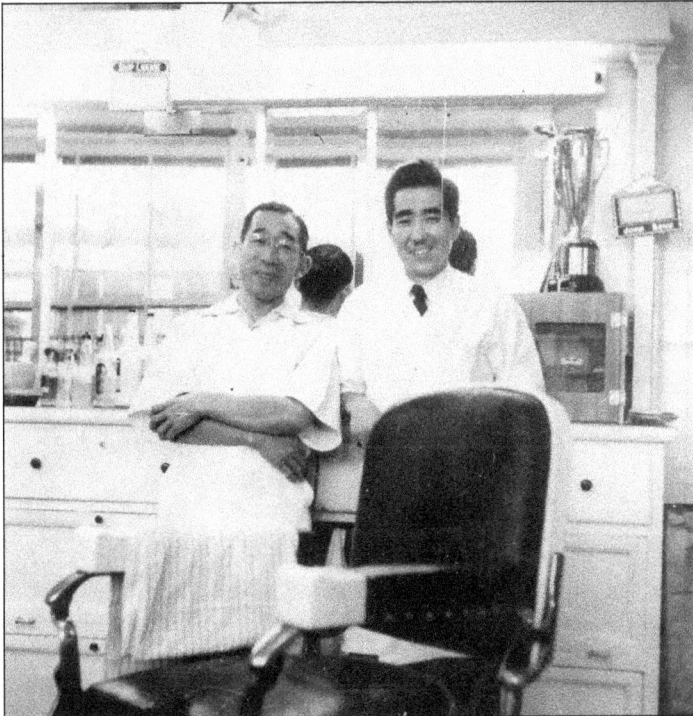

Pictured around 1948 inside Roy's Barbershop at 1620 Laguna Street are Roy Abe and John Kono. (Courtesy of JAHA/JCCCNC.)

The American Fish Market reopened after the war and moved to this location at the corner of Buchanan and Sutter Streets, where business continued until new ownership, now a Super Mira Market. (Courtesy of Greg Marutani.)

The Walter-McCarran Immigration and Nationality Act passes in 1952, enabling Asians immigrants to become naturalized citizens of the United States. Many became citizens shortly thereafter at naturalization ceremonies such as this one held at the San Francisco City Hall in 1952. (Courtesy of JANL.)

Honnami Taieido was one of the first Japanese American businesses to open after the internment. The business began as a general merchandise store, but gradually specialized in Japanese art goods. Pictured inside are Suwa Honnami, Hikoroku Honnami, Leslie Taniguchi, Alan Taniguchi, Taeko Nagano, and Sumi Honnami. (Courtesy of Sumi Honnami.)

In the 1930s, Azumaya Tofu Factory manufactured fresh tofu and related products in Japantown. Started above Uoki K. Sakai on Post Street, Azumaya Tofu moved to Geary Street near Buchanan Street by 1940 and returned there after World War II. They were forced out by redevelopment in 1959 to an industrial zone on Third Street and went on to become a national presence. Pictured in the middle of this family photograph are Matsuyo and Saichi Mizono, c. 1955 (Courtesy of Arrice Mizono Mori.)

Wallace "Wally" Kaname Yonamine, a *Nisei* born in Hawaii, was generally considered the Jim Thorpe of the Japanese Americans. Drafted straight from high school, he played professional football for the San Francisco 49ers in 1947. (Courtesy of NJAHS.)

The YWCA auditorium at 1530 Buchanan Street was the scene of this 1955 dance. (Courtesy of JAHA/JCCCNC.)

1956

to Downtown

Buddhist Churh of SF
St. Francis Xavier Catholic Church
Morning Star Catholic School
(1 block northeast)

Soko Mission
(Soto Zen Buddhist)
Nippon Ki-in Soko Shibu
(Go Club)

K.F. Drayage

Miyako Barber Shop
Alice Beauty Shop
Jim's Drug

Mike's Richfield Service (1 block)

Roy's Barber Shop

Seiki   Naganuma &
Plumber Son Plumber

Yamato Auto Repairing
Dobashi Fishing Tackle
Wong's Bait Shop

Miyako
Barber
Shop

Japanese Church of
Christ (Presbyterian)
(1 block east)

Yanase Florist

Kinmon Press

CEDAR STREET

Tomahiro Art

Salvation Army

LAGUNA STREET

Hotel
Kirkland

Konkokyo Church
Konkokyo Gakuen
School

Coast Camera & Radio

Kinoshita
Apartments

United Enterprises
James S. Hirano
Shima Transfer Draying Co.

Nippon Fish
Goldfish Ponds
Co.

Miyako Jeweler

Japan Trading Co.

HEMLOCK STREET

Laguna Chowa
Kenko-kai
Honbu

Kono's Barber Shop
Hyotan Band

Hosoi Embroidery

Hokkubei Mainichi
Newspaper/ Printing
M. Onuma, Notary

Japanese American
Citizen's League
Soko Nichibei-Kai
Taiyo Kawai Amusements
Oriental Culture Book Co.
Sowan Ma Jong League

Seiki Bros.
Plumbing/
Appliances

Tiger Cafe
Tokyo Parlor Rest.
Taiyo Trading Co.
Murata Insurance
Yoshida Insurance

Hosada Brothers
Food Import/Export

Nisei Barber Shop
Nisei Fishing Club

Shirlen
Apartments

Victor Abe Law Office/ Notary
Baba Urin Ikenobo, Sakai, DDS Tani Shoe
Post Market & Fishing Tackle Repairing
Motonari Chiryo-In   Soko Engeie-Kai
Hideshima Employment Agency
Post Pool Room
Aki Hotel Travel Service

Takahashi Trading Co. Art Goods
Takanega Chiryo-In

T. Takeda Painter
Post Shoe Repairing

Ginza Sukiyaki
Mikado Grill

China Chop Suey
Restaurant

Zalman Co.

Nankaiya Hotel
Tokyo Bath House

Hokubei Hotel

Dr. K. J.
Kitagawa
T. Tsunato
D.D.S.

Japanese American
Hotel Association of SF
Japanese Dental Association

Buchanan YMCA

Isoye Hand
Embroidery

Shima Transfer
& Drayage Co.

American Fish Market

C.T. Hirota, Dentist
Koga Co. Grocery
& Fountain

Hisago Restaurant
Mary's Beauty Salon

Evergreen Fountain
Nakamura Tailor
Modern Watch
Shop

Soo Chow
Restaurant

Uoki K. Sakai
Grocery
Jimbo's Bop City

Soko
Hardware

Fuji Hotel
Fuji Framing
Tempura House
Murata Kurotori
Notary & Insurance
Yamato Masso

BUCHANAN STREET

M. Itatani Optometrist
Japanese Limousine Service
JA Book Dealers Association

Mikado Hotel
Nakagawa
Gosha-Do Books

Five Star
Fountain
Hideshima
Employment
Agency

N.B. Department Store
(Nichibei Bussan)

Lucky Bait Shop

Kinmon
Bookstore

Jack's Employment Agency
Y. Fujita DDS

S. Horio MD

Marino
Brothers
Grocery

Matsuye Florist

Miyako Restaurant

K Y Liquors
Honnami Taiedo Art Goods
Pioneer Radio & TV
Minakin Restaurant
Nippon Pool Room
Jimmy's Barber Shop

Sanko Shoji Co.
Minato Shokudo
Restaurant

Benkyo-Do Co.

Azumaya Tofu Co.

Hori Employment Agency
Otafuko-Tei Restaurant

Kinmon Gakuen
(Golden Gate School)

Hokka Judo
Nihon Eiga-bu Movies

Japanese YWCA
American Friends
Service Committee

Kumano
Apartments

Handa Contractor

Kume
Apartments

BUSH STREET

SUTTER STREET

POST STREET

S.F. Independent Church
Mt Pilgrim Baptist Church
(1957-'74)

New Crescent Hotel
Kawal Travel Service

SUNNY CT.

GEARY STREET

Mizuhara Art Repair

Yoshiko Beauty Salon
Umeboko Kyu Institute

Fuji Hotel
Fujiona Haton

WEBSTER STREET

Geary Cafe
Vi's Beauty
Shop

Redevelopment Area A-1

Soko Engenkai

DEMOLISHED FOR JAPAN CENTER 1959-1961

DEMOLISHED FOR GEARY EXPRESSWAY 1959-1961

Yamamoto Liberty Cleaners

Shimada Hotel
Apartments

Ace
Restaurant

SAN FRANCISCO

MARKET

VAN NESS

FILLMORE   Japantown

GEARY

N

Sanborn map data ©EDR, used by permission.

Hedani
Optometrist
Takeo Okamoto
Insurance

Royal Paint &
Wallpaper

California Cleaners to Pacific Heights
Tokyo Fish Market
Sueyasu Wholesale Florist

Les & Yo's Mobil Service
Uptown Garage
(1 block)

Big Glass Tavern

FILLMORE STREET

to Richmond District
& Cliff House

Fillmore Auditorium/
Majestic Hall

This map shows the location of Japantown businesses in 1956. (Courtesy of Ben Pease.)

In 1960, Mr. Tokioka, a developer, presented plans for the new Japanese Cultural and Trade Center to the Japanese consul general and Justin Herman, San Francisco Redevelopment Director (seated). This three-block complex displaced 50 businesses and 1500 residents, and was part of the larger 27-block redevelopment phase. Construction began in 1965 and completed in 1968. (Courtesy of San Francisco Redevelopment Agency.)

The Geary Expressway and the Japan Center, under construction, are seen during the mid 1960s. After years of planning, negotiations, and delay, the Japan Center rises from the vacant blocks. (Courtesy of JANL.)

The A-2 phase of redevelopment (north of Post Street) involved the displacement of property owners and cultural institutions. In the Western Addition, 11,000 units of low-cost housing were destroyed and replaced with only 7,132 units of affordable housing. Citizens Against Nihon machi Evictions (CANE) was organized in 1973 to decry the loss of affordable housing and the destruction of neighborhood businesses to make tourist-oriented hotels and shops. (Courtesy of JANL.)

CANE's first newsletter, Volume 1 No. 1, came out in July/August 1973. The cover art was designed by Jack Matsuoka. (Courtesy of JANL.)

The Japan Center nears completion (1967–1968) in this view that also shows the 16-story Miyako Hotel and the foundation for the Peace Pagoda (foreground). (Courtesy of JANL.)

Here is a 1968 inside view of the Kintesu Mall of the Japan Center. (Courtesy of San Francisco Redevelopment Agency.)

1970

to Downtown

GEARY EXPRESSWAY

Salvation Army
(sold 1974 to
Chinese Consulate)

Buddhist Church of SF
St. Francis Xavier Catholic Church
Morning Star Catholic School
(1 block northeast)

Soto Zen Temple
American Legion Post 438
Nippon Ki-in (Go Club)

K.F. Drayage

Jimmy's Barber Shop
Marcie's Beauty Salon
Jefferson Cleaners
Hatani Optometrist

Naganuma Plumber

Yamato Auto Repair
Wong's Bait & Tackle

Hosoda Brothers
Grocery/Import/Export

Roy's Barber Shop
Sowan Majong League

Japanese Church of
Christ (Presbyterian)
Girl Scout Troops
257, 197, 57, 37-1
(1 block east)

Weldon
Grocery
CANE

LAGUNA STREET

Kinmon Camera Club
Sowan Kagoshima Kenjin-Kai
Hiroshima Nikkeijin-Kai
Shinsei Band

Kyo's Knitting
Machine

Konkokyo
Church of SF

Nippon
Goldfish
Co.

Boy Scout
Troop 58

Inoye Hand
Embroidery

Coast Camera & Radio TV

Kinoshita
Apartments
Sumi Fishing Tackle

SUTTER PLACE

American Fish Market

Teru Togasaki, M.D.

Nippon & America
Editorial Offices

Den's Auto
Service

HEMLOCK

Japan Trading Co.
Kono's Barber Shop
Mimatsu Restaurant

Seiki Brothers
Hardware, Plumbing & Appliance
Club Kyoto (Bar)

JACL National Headquarters
Kyoto Laundrette
House of Imports
Imperial Imports

Hokubei Mainichi
Newspaper/Printing

Uoki K. Sakai Co.
Japanese Grocery

Japanese American Assn. of SF
JACL of SF

Oriental Culture Book Store
Naturalization School

Fuji Electronic Service

Soo Chow Low
Restaurant

Gosha-Do
Books & Art Goods

Nisei Barber Shop
Soko Hardware

Hisago Japanese Rest.

Mary's Beauty Salon

Nichibei Bussan
Department Store
Evergreen Fountain

Yano Hardwood Floor

POST STREET

EAST BUILDING

Consulate General of Japan
Japan Emigration Service

Japanese
Garden

Miyako Hotel
(Kintetsu Enterprises)

Miyako Hotel
Barber Shop &
Beauty Salon

Meeting
Rooms

Miyako Hotel
Entry Court

Jim's
Drugs

Sakurayi
Restaurant

Kabuki
Cocktails

2nd
Floor

Bank of Tokyo

Additional Businesses
(Locations Not Specified)
Aki Travel Service
Bonsai by Kay
Ginza Barber
Ginza Bazaar
Ichiban Shop
Sino Jewelry
Edoya (Food/Confections)
Jakima Palace of Cards
U-N-O Trading Co.
Paper Tree Stationery
Pinocchio Children's Shop
Rovere Bridge Club
SF Federal Savings & Loan
Showa Travel Service
T. Okamoto Insurance
Thai Thai Boutique
Zen Hair Styles
Kyo's Jewelry

Buchanan YWCA

BUCHANAN STREET

Japanese Cultural & Trade Center

PEACE PLAZA

Peace
Pagoda

Pool

Pool

Pool

ST. FRANCIS SQUARE COOPERATIVE APARTMENTS

BUSH STREET

Redevelopment Area A-2

Takeshita Silk
Mounting Studio

future Kyoto Inn (1974)
(today's Miyako Inn)

Kinmon Gakuen
(Golden Gate School)
Soko Judo Dojo

YWCA

Kumano Apts

Kume Apts

SUTTER STREET

Benkyodo Co.

Otafuke-Tei Restaurant
Fuji-ya Gifts, Books, Art Goods
Radio New Japan

Eddie Ichiro Moriguchi Accountant/Tax

Toraya Apartments
Ricksha Realty
Toraya Restaurant

S. Handa Sons
Building Contractor

Mount Pilgrim
Missionary
Baptist Church
(1956-1974)

Sowan Tottori Kenjin-Kai
Homami Taido
Art Goods

Nishiki
Cocktail Lounge

Miyako Restaurant

future Nihonmachi Bldg
& Kokusai Theater (1971)

KINTETSU CENTER

Japantown Bowl (1974-2000)

Nissan Motors
Datsun Auto
Showroom

Kinki Nippon Tourist Co.
(Kintetsu Travel)

Japan National
Tourist Org. JNTO

Hitatchi Ltd.
Showroom

Mikado
Gift Shop

Suehiro
Restaurant

Misa's
Boutique

Ohja Cocktail Lounge

Mitsubishi
Exhibition
Center

Additional Businesses
(Locations Not Specified)
Niagara Cyclo-Massage
Oyster Pearl Display
Tokyo Electronics
O-Cha-Ya

Miseki
Jewelry

Ikenoko

Ikebana

Makiya
Florist

Gallery
Kabukiya

Murata
Pearls

K.Y. Liquors

pedestrian bridge

Kam Ling Rest.

Gallery-Do
Overseas
Trading Co.

WEBSTER STREET

Redevelopment Area A-2
Redevelopment Area A-1

Ishi's Mobil
Service

Kintaki Shokado
Restaurant

WEST BUILDING

Kinokuniya
Bookstore

2nd
Floor

Additional Businesses
(Locations Not Specified)
Osaka-ya Restaurant
George Yamazaki
Bar Kabuki
Rika Jewelry
Gallery Do
Shinjuku Bar
Tomiko Bar
Naris Cosmetics
House of Pillows
Kiosk Corp. of America
Kikoman Cooking Center
Kikkoman International
Crocker-Citizens National Bank
Kintetsu Enterprises of America
National-Braemar (Mall Developers)

Tajima Architect
Sano Interpreter

Restaurant Kabuki
Bar Kabuki

Kabuki Theatre

Kabuki Onsen
(Japanese Baths)

The Nippon & America
News/Books/Stationery

Kawatomi
Japanese Rest.

Medani
Optometrist

California Cleaners
Tokyo Fish Market   to Pacific Heights
Toraya Restaurant
& several others (1 block)

(Nichi Bei Times Newspaper
moved in 1974 from Eddy Street)
Uptown Garage
Les & Yo's Mobil Service

FILLMORE STREET

to Richmond District
& Cliff House

Filmore
Auditorium

SAN FRANCISCO

MARKET
VAN NESS
Japantown
FILLMORE
GEARY

N

Sanborn map data ©EDR, used by permission.

In 1970, this is the way Japantown looked. (Courtesy of Ben Pease.)

83

The Buchanan Mall's "River of Cobblestones" was a collaboration of landscape architect and planner Rai Okamoto and artist Ruth Asawa. Ruth Asawa designed the two origami fountains, fabricated of steel to resemble traditional folded paper flower designs. She also designed the benches, with clay art sculpted by local school children and cast in concrete. The mall retains much of the playfulness and creativity of these artists. (Courtesy of Sumi Honnami.)

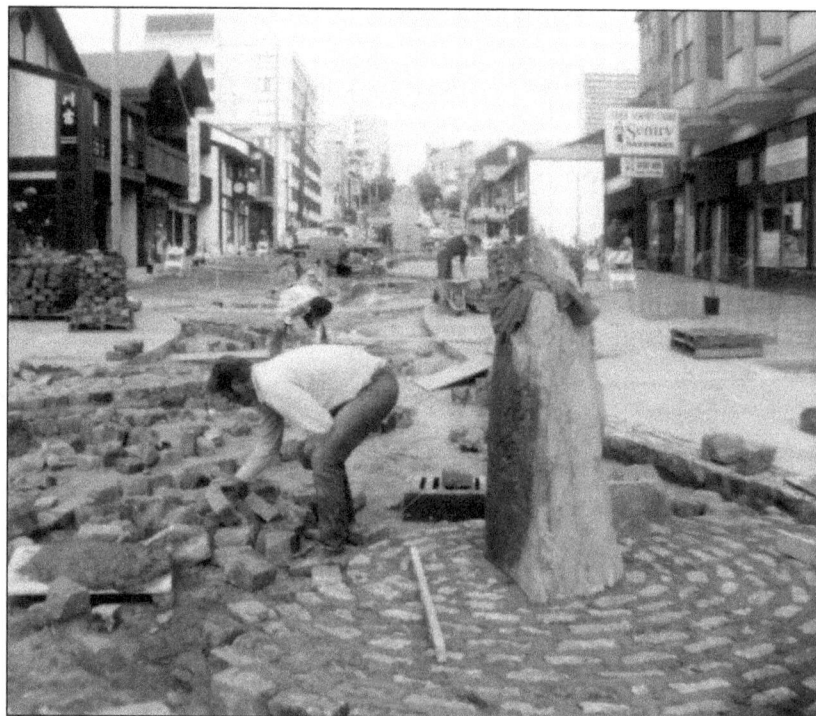

Construction of Buchanan Mall is progressing in this 1975 photograph. (Courtesy of Sumi Honnami.)

In March 1976, a Konko-Kyo priest performs the ritual cleansing of Buchanan Mall during its dedication. In background is the former postwar location of the Tatsuno family's Nichibei Bussan department store—the old Victorian dwelling neatly draped with a contemporary wooden screen. Nichibei Bussan moved across the street and in its place was Honnami Taieido, which was displaced from Sutter Street by the new Miyako Inn. (Courtesy of Sumi Honnami.)

The Buchanan Mall Gate is one of the most visible cultural landmarks in Japantown. During the mid 1960s, Rai Okamoto began to develop a master plan in conjunction with the SFRA to create a major public works project on the Buchanan Plaza. The gate was finished along with the rest of the Buchanan Plaza in 1976. (Courtesy of San Francisco Redevelopment Agency.)

The view up Buchanan Mall towards Post Street and the Japan Trade and Cultural Center from one of the origami fountains. (Courtesy of San Francisco Redevelopment Agency.)

A view of the Nichibei Bussan department store on Buchanan Mall. (Courtesy of San Francisco Redevelopment Agency.)

Pictured is one of two origami fountains on Buchanan Mall. (Courtesy of San Francisco Redevelopment Agency.)

Hokubei Mainchi was established in 1948 to serve the Japanese American population in the Northern California area. The newspaper is currently one of only two remaining bilingual Japanese-English newspapers in the entire Bay Area, with distribution in the several thousands. Pictured is the newspaper building when it was located on Sutter Street. It is presently at 1746 Post Street. (Courtesy of Greg Marutani.)

Howard Imazeki worked for the *Hokubei Mainchi* newspaper for over 25 years as the English editor and president. He is pictured here around 1977 working on the layout of the paper. (Courtesy of Joyce Yamamoto.)

In November 1972, *Nichi Bei Times* general manager Tsutomu Umezu greets visitors at the open house of their new building at 2211 Bush Street. Pictured here, from left to right, are Tokyo Bank chairman Masao Tsuyama, San Francisco supervisor Quentin Kopp, California State Senator Milton Marks, noted artist Chiura Obata, Umezu, unidentified, Motoo Iratani, *Nichi Bei Times* Fresno branch manager Masao Araki, *Nichi Bei* president Shichinosuke Asano, architect David Asano, unidentified, and Mas Ashizawa. (Courtesy of *Nichi Bei Times*.)

On May 18, 1946, *Nichi Bei Times*, Northern California's oldest Japanese American bilingual daily newspaper, rolled off the presses. Some of the prewar staff of the *Nichi Bei Shimbun* (founded in 1899 by Kyutaro Abiko) returned to form the *Nichi Bei Times*. First located at 1775 Sutter Street, the newspaper moved to 1375 Eddy Street due to redevelopment. Their current location is on Bush Street. (Courtesy of *Nichi Bei Times*.)

The family-run business, Benkyodo Manju Company, remains one of the oldest business in Japantown. Hirofumi Okamura (center) operated the store for 30 years before his sons Bobby (left) and Ricky (right) took over. (Courtesy of Bobby Okamura.)

In 1973, Kintetsu hired May Murata to run their coffee shop in the Japan Center. It was small and had a limited menu of Japanese food and *sembi* (rice crackers). In 1985, the name was changed to May's Coffee Shop and the shop expanded. Now operated by her daughter Pearl, the menu includes spam musubi, teri burgers, and saimin. (Courtesy of May Murata.)

Five

COMMUNITY SPIRIT AND CELEBRATION

Cultural pride and celebrations are the core to San Francisco's Japantown. The two largest public events, the Cherry Blossom Festival held in the spring and the *Nihonmachi* Street Fair held each August, attracts thousands each year. Other events, organizations, and demonstrations focused on *Nikkei* heritage contributes to an ongoing way of life.

Numerous community-based organizations (CBOs) serve generations of families and businesses in Japantown. These CBOs fill the spiritual, educational, social, and activist needs.

In the late 1960s, with the creation of the Ethnic Studies Program at San Francisco State University and the beginning of the Asian American political movement, the evolution of Japantown's nonprofit, community-based service organizations began.

The *Sansei* (third-generation Japanese Americans) promoted their ethnic identity as Japanese Americans. Observing the disenfranchisement created by the void in culturally sensitive services, *Sansei* saw the need for alternative, ethnically based services and formed many grassroots organizations based in Japantown to serve the needs of both Japantown residents and the extended Japanese American community.

Annual community picnics were held in Golden Gate Park. Pictured at the 1975 event, from left to right, are (first row) Yo Hironaka, Marcia Hironaka, Jack Hirose, and Fumi Hoshiyama; (second row) Kiyo Hirose, Amey Aizawa, Hanako Yamane, Elaine Yamane, and Hats Aizawa. (Courtesy of Aizawa family.)

Mrs. Haru Baba (second row, far right) founded the first Japanese American Brownie Girl Scout troop in 1947. They met at the Reform Church on Post Street. (Courtesy of Ayako Nishimoto.)

The Christ United Presbyterian Church Girl Scout Troop No. 37 is seen here c. 1957. (Courtesy of Ayako Nishimoto.)

Around 1959, a group of Cub Scouts posed for this photograph. (Courtesy of Doug Inouye)

A March 1956 photograph shows Boy Scout Troop No. 29. (Courtesy of Doug Inouye.)

On June 1, 1940, Boy Scout Troop No. 12 celebrates its 25th anniversary. (Courtesy of Will Tsukamoto.)

Boy Scout Troop No. 12's drum and bugle corps march in the annual Cherry Blossom Parade. (Courtesy of Yukiko Tanaka.)

Organized in 1918, the San Francisco Nisei Fishing Club's purpose is to promote the interest of the younger generation in outdoor sports such as hunting, fishing. It also teaches the values of conservation and preservation of the wonder of nature. (Courtesy of Nisei Fishing Club.)

In 1969, young anglers pose for a group photograph at the Huck Finn outing at Lake Berryessa. (Courtesy of Nisei Fishing Club.)

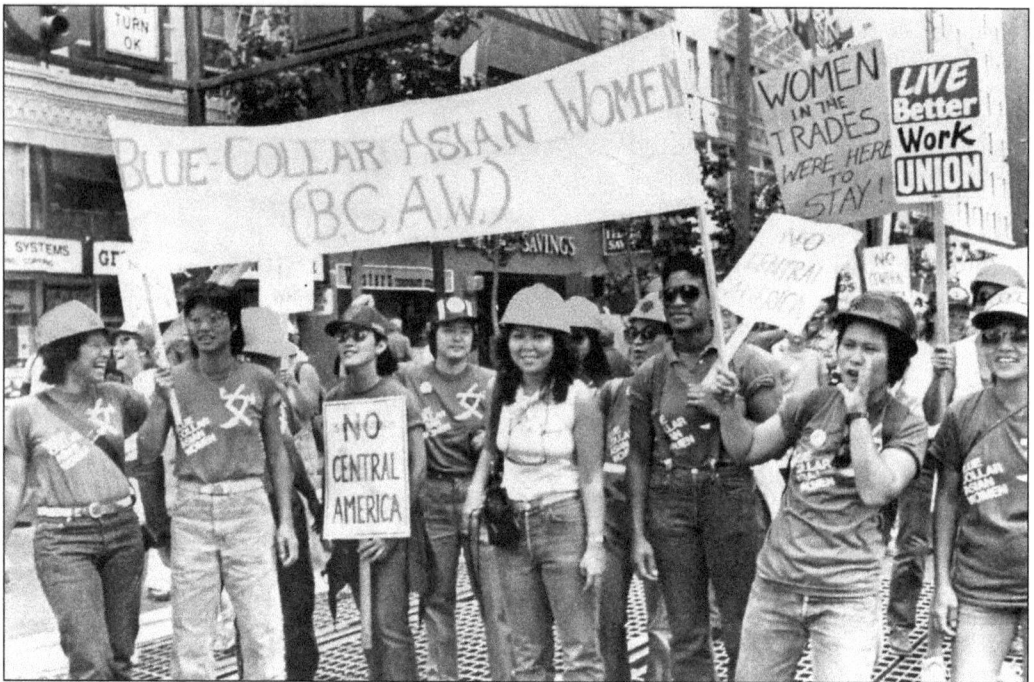

In 1984, Linda Jofuku (center, white shirt) and the Blue Collar Asian Women participate in the Two-Headed Dragon rally to protest the Two-Gate policy. This policy allowed both union and non-union workers at construction sites. (Courtesy of NJAHS.)

In 1977, the International Hotel on Kearny Street was the site of widespread community protest resulting in the eviction of 100 low-income housing tenants. Eventually under the ownership of the San Francisco Catholic Archdiocese and others, after 28 years, it is now low-income housing again. (Courtesy of JANL.)

In 1996, the San Francisco YWCA decided to sell the historical building designed in 1932 by world-renowned architect Julia Morgan, at commercial rates beyond the reach of community organizations. The Soko Bukai, the organization of Japanese Christian Churches, filed suit to enforce the documented trust agreement. In 2002, Nihonmachi Little Friends was able to purchase the property and become the owner of the building. (Above photograph courtesy of San Francisco Public Library, History Center; below photograph courtesy of Nihonmachi Little Friends.)

When the Kintetsu Company announced it would close its popular recreational facility in the summer of 2000, the community (particularly youth and seniors) rallied to try to keep the 40-lane Japantown Bowl. Despite community offers for the property, including maintaining it as a bowling alley, Kintetsu closed the facility on September 20, 2000, and eventually sold the property to developers for mostly market-rate housing and commercial space. (Courtesy of *Nichi Bei Times*.)

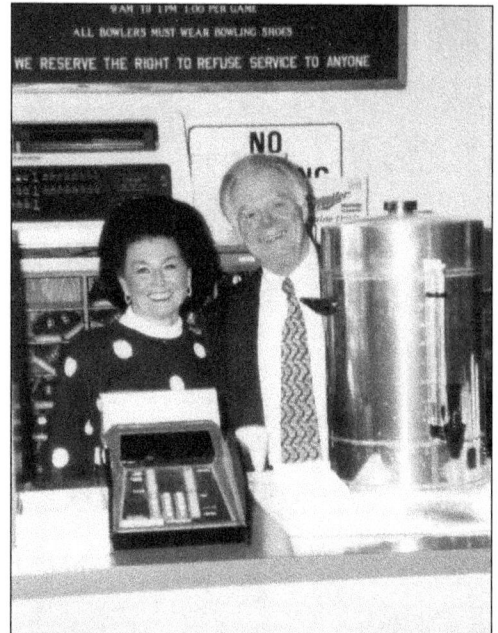

Robert Hirano, left, pickets the closure of Japantown Bowl. Japantown Bowl managers Edith DeFlorio and Bert Webb, right, give smiles from behind the counter. (Left courtesy of Chris Hirano; right courtesy of Calvert Kitazumi.)

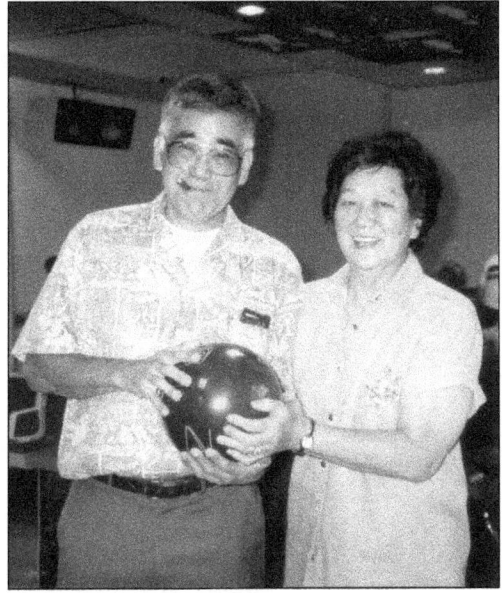

Sanji Fukuyama, above left, voluntarily arranged monthly bus trips for the senior residents of Hinode Towers and others to Reno, Sacramento, and other places within California. Sanji, pictured at left in 1987, was an avid bowler at Japantown Bowl. Calvert and Betty Kitazumi, right, pose for a photograph during their regular bowling night at Japantown Bowl. (Courtesy of Calvert Kitazumi.)

Here is the 1954 Simmons bowling team. (Courtesy of Nunotani family.)

Sokoji Temple, a Zen Buddhist temple founded in 1934, was originally housed in the Jewish Synagogue building at 1881 Bush Street (now Kokoro Assisted Living). In 1984, a new building was completed and dedicated. In 2004, the 70th anniversary of the Soto Mission of San Francisco and Sokoji Rev. Kiko Tatedera's installation ceremony was celebrated. (Courtesy of Soto Mission, Sokoji Zen Temple.)

Founded in 1898, the San Francisco Buddhist Church is the oldest congregation of the Buddhist Churches of America. This building was constructed in 1935, and features include a stupa (hidden behind tree) to house ashes of the Buddha, given to the BCA by the emperor of Siam (Thailand). (Courtesy of Misako Mori.)

The Nichiren Buddhist Church, located at 2016 Pine Street, is pictured here. (Courtesy of Misako Mori.)

Founded in 1948 as *Shukyoka Konwakai*, the Japanese American Religious Federation (JARF) fosters better relationships among religious leaders in the community. In 1975, Nihonmachi Terrace was built, a housing complex for seniors and low-income families. In the 1990s, JARF also assisted in the construction of Kokoro Assisted Living Center, a 54-unit facility for ailing seniors. Federation members are seen during the eight-year anniversary of the Japanese Christian Mission (later renamed JARF). (Courtesy of Rev. Richard Grange.)

The Konko-Kyo Church was founded in 1930 by Rev. Yoshiaki Fukuda, and is currently located at 1909 Bush Street. During World War II, the FBI classified Rev. Fukuda as a Class-A Japanese leader and was interned for almost six years, forcing the church to close. Pictured is the grand ceremony conducted by Rev. Fukuda (far right). (Courtesy of Rev. Richard Grange, Konko-Kyo Church.)

The 25th anniversary of the Konko-Kyo Church is celebrated in 1956. (Courtesy of Rev. Richard Grange, Konko-Kyo Church.)

Pictured here, members of the Seinen Kai youth group at a 1950s beach outing are, from left to right, Mitsuko Nakahara, William Nakahara, Wataru Nakahara, unidentified, Sumako Takeshita, Kenji Takeshita, Eiji Ayabe, and two unidentified. (Courtesy of Rev. Richard Grange, Konko-Kyo Church of San Francisco.)

Members of the First Evangelical and Reform Church gather for a group photograph. (Courtesy Dr. Himeo Tsumori.)

The *Nihonjin-Machi* Japanese Catholic community began in 1913. Fr. Albert Breton, M.M., established a church at 2158 Pine Street. In 1929, Father Stoecke established Morning Star School, an elementary school that taught Japanese language. Father Stoecke went to Topaz to minister to the Japanese parishioners until 1945. In 1993, St. Benedict Parish for the Deaf merged with the church. Pictured are members of the sign-language class. (Courtesy of Sumi Honnami.)

On April 18, 1976, the Christ United Presbyterian congregation gathers to commemorate the new church built in 1975 at the corner of Sutter and Laguna Streets. (Courtesy of Christ United Presbyterian Church.)

For 23 years, Japantown Arts and Media (JAM) provided a creative outlet for the Bay Area Asian American community. It was a group of talented artists who were drawn together by their love of both art and their community. The Taniguchis show off a JAM designed T-shirt at Nihonmachi Street Fair. (Courtesy of and JAHA/JCCCNC.)

Nobiru-Kai, Japanese Newcomer Services, was founded in 1974 and provides bilingual/bicultural community services to Japanese citizens who are new arrivals to the San Francisco Bay Area. (Courtesy of Nobiru-Kai.)

Brought together by an interest in bonsai, the San Francisco Bonsai Society was founded in 1970 by *Kibei*, second-generation Japanese Americans who were educated in Japan. Many in the society are gardeners or landscapers by trade. (Courtesy of Johnny Nagano.)

As the original school of Ikebana in Japan, Ikenobo, the art of arranging flowers, has a long history of over 550 years. After World War II, there were many followers who expressed the desire to continue the study of Ikenobo Ikebana. In 1968, answering that need, the 45th-generation Headmaster Sen'ei Ikenobo, established a San Francisco office, including two visiting residents professors from Japan each year. Pictured is Louise Ow Ling. (Courtesy of Misako Mori.)

This is a 1960s Nikkei Lions Club annual dinner event. (Courtesy of JANL.)

Yori Wada, the first Japanese and Asian American appointed to the Board of Regents for the University of California and director of the Buchanan Street YMCA, was a long-standing community advocate. He is photographed helping with the JCCCNC yaki soba concession at the 1987 Cherry Blossom Festival. (Courtesy of Chiyo Wada.)

Founded in 1973, the Japanese Cultural and Community Center of Northern California (JCCCNC) is a 17,500 square foot facility providing a multitude of cultural, educational, recreational, and social programs. (Courtesy of Misako Mori.)

Since 1971, Kimochi, Incorporated has developed and promoted an intergenerational philosophy of care for seniors and families. *"Kimochi"* means "feelings" in Japanese, referring to feelings of respect and concern for the older generations. Started by a few *Sansei* (third generation), they realized language and cultural barriers prevented many elderly *Issei* (first generation) from accessing mainstream social services. Pictured (center) is Steve Nakajo, executive director. (Courtesy of Kimochi Center.)

Built in 1895, the Kokoro building was once a Jewish synagogue, the Congregation Ohabai Shalom Temple, and the Japanese Soto Zen Buddhist Church before its renovation was completed in 2003. It is now the Kokoro Assisted Living Center. (Courtesy of Misako Mori.)

residents, family, and staff gathered at the Hamilton Senior Center for this 1968 photograph. (Courtesy of Hamilton Senior Center.)

The Japanese American National Library was established in 1969 in response to a demand from the San Francisco State University Admissions Department. When students and faculty set out to create ethnic studies as an accredited program, SFSU demanded a curriculum with specific details and references. Pictured is Karl Matsushita, the library's director. (Courtesy of Misako Mori.)

Every weekday, June-ko Nakagawa broadcasts to more than 10,000 listeners across the Bay Area. San Francisco Radio Mainichi began over 15 years ago as a weekly radio broadcast for native Japanese speakers and is currently the first and only Japanese radio station in Northern California. In June 2004, San Francisco Radio Mainichi was officially recognized by Japan's foreign minister for its service in aiding Japanese-American relations. (Courtesy of Misako Mori.)

The National Japanese American Historical Society was founded as Go For Broke, Inc. in 1980 to inform the public about the military history of the *Nisei* soldier. In 1983, the organization changed to its current name to reflect a broader purpose. Pictured is Peter Yamamoto showing one of the current exhibits. (Courtesy of Misako Mori.)

Until 2004, Seizo Oka managed the Japanese American History Archives. The collection was created in 1977 by the California First Bank (now Union Bank) and continued to grow with items donated by members of the community or procured by Oka, a retired vice president of the bank. The collection was donated by California First Bank to the Japanese Cultural and Community Center of Northern California. (Courtesy of Keith Oka/JAHA/JCCCNC.)

Richard Griffith, mayor of San Bruno, is speaking to the audience at the first Day of Remembrance (1979) to commemorate President Roosevelt's authorization of Executive Order 9066 and the evacuation and internment of over 120,000 people of Japanese ancestry in 1942. (Courtesy of Isao Isago Tanaka/NJAHS.)

In 1979, Janice Mirikitani, Rev. Cecil Williams, and Hiroshi Kashiwagi attend the first Day of Remembrance observance at Tanforan Racetrack in San Bruno. (Courtesy of NJAHS.)

In 1969, a group of Japanese American youth organized a youth council with the purpose of addressing issues impacting young people. The need for a facility was identified and a vacant two-story building, located on Sutter Street, evolved into a multiservice community center. The Japanese Community Youth Council was officially incorporated in May 1970 as a nonprofit organization serving the youth from all socioeconomic and ethnic backgrounds. (Courtesy of JCYC.)

The Others, a local band comprised of members of the San Francisco Junior JACL, pose for a photograph. Pictured c. 1966, from left to right, are Russell Baba, Larry Morino, Glenn Watanabe, and Ken Shimamoto. (Courtesy of George Okada.)

Successful businessman and community leader Takeo Okamoto established T. Okamoto and Company in 1947, specializing in insurance and real estate. Kay Okamoto was also active in various organizations in Japantown. The couple is pictured celebrating their 40th wedding anniversary. (Courtesy of Pat Okamoto.)

Tak Matsuba, Optimist Club president, presented awards to the Sunset Jets team, Pee Wee A-league champions, c. 1992 (Courtesy of the Optimist Club.)

Edison Uno, a quiet, slender San Francisco State University professor, was known for his turtlenecks and his passion for justice. Uno was a visionary who successfully protested in favor of the integration of the San Francisco grand jury, fought for guaranteed jobs and medical care, and hammered the JACL to fight a long-overdue justice to seek redress for Japanese Americans. In 1970, the National Council of the JACL finally adopted a resolution to seek redress and reparations. (Courtesy of Isao Isago Tanaka/NJAHS.)

In 2002, members of the San Francisco VFW Golden Gate Post No. 9879 Ladies Auxiliary pose in front of a streetcar. (Courtesy of the Nunotani family.)

On May 23, 1998, alums from the Center for Japanese American Studies gather for a retrospective photograph. The center hosts lectures and symposiums to gain greater knowledge of educational issues impacting the Japanese American communities. (Courtesy of JANL.)

In 1993, Troop No. 29 Boy Scouts continue the tradition of pushing a large daruma in the annual Cherry Blossom parade. Pictured here, from left to right, are Gary Kishida, two unidentified, Erik Satow, Sean Yakota, and two unidentified. (Courtesy of Doug Inouye.)

Women and girls, dressed in traditional kimonos, gather prior to the start of the first Cherry Blossom parade in 1967. (Courtesy of Nunotani family.)

Veterans of Foreign War Golden Gate Nisei Memorial Post No. 9879 color guard parades down Post Street in the Cherry Blossom parade.

The 1971 Cherry Blossom queen, Nancy Kaoru (Matsumoto) Seino, accepts a city proclamation from Mayor Joseph Alioto, an unidentified samuari, and George Yamasaki Jr. (Courtesy of JANL.)

Grand Marshals for the 1968 Cherry Blossom parade are Motoji Kitano (front), Soichii Nakatani (back left), and Shichinosuke Asano. (Courtesy of Jean Nakatani Yego.)

Parade participants help to hoist and carry the Taru Mikoshi—an altar of wooden sake barrels, weighing about one-and-a-half tons, to close out the Cherry Blossom Parade. The Taru Mikoshi has been carried in the parade for over 37 years. This photograph from 1974 has Sensei Seiichi Tanaka and Nosuke Akiyama. Another tradition following the parade is the annual soak at the Kabuki Hot Springs. (Courtesy of San Francisco Taiko Dojo.)

Obon is a summer tradition that began in Japan centuries ago. It's a time when people honor loved ones who have passed on during the year. Every year, Buddhist temples hold *obon* services and *bon-odori* (dancing) with tradition dances, music, and kimonos. In the mid-1960s, the dancing took place on Buchanan Street (today's Buchanan Mall). (Courtesy of San Francisco Redevelopment Agency.)

It is believed that *koinobori*, colorful carp streamers, will bring good fortune to children. *Koinobori* are strong, spirited fish who show determination when fighting upstream. Every May 5, carp streamers fly above the Peace Plaza to celebrate *Tango no Sekku* or Boys Day. (Courtesy of JANL.)

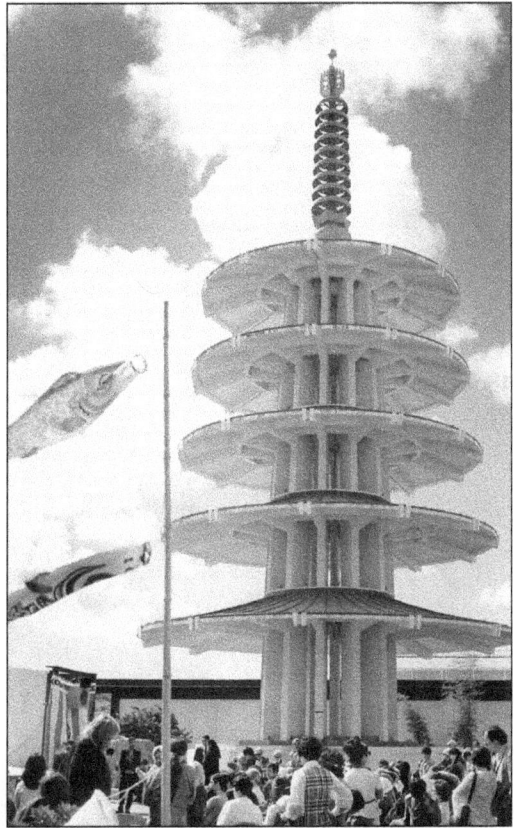

Families display *kabuto* (samurai helmets) and samurai dolls such as *kintaro* and *momotaro* to symbolize courage. Pictured is Masahiko Nakata during the 1932 *Tango no Sekku* (Boys Day). (Courtesy of Himeo Tsumori.)

中田政彦 昭和六年七月十九日生
昭和七年五月五日之写
may. 5 1932 By SHTO
55

Seiichi Tanaka began the San Francisco Taiko Dojo in 1968, the first such organized group in the United States. Grand master Tanaka and the San Francisco Taiko Dojo have collaborated and performed with a diverse lineup of luminaries in the music industry. Such musicians include Tony Bennett, Bobby McFerrin, the original Temptations, Dave Brubeck, Art Blakey, Tito Puente, Mickey Hart, Mario Bauza, Max Roach, and Kitaro. (Courtesy of San Francisco Taiko Dojo.)

The San Francisco Taiko Dojo has gained world wide attention with their performances in many countries. Notable performances include Carnegie Hall, for Emperor Hirohito, and at the Hiroshima 50th commemoration ceremony in Japan. Pictured in 1998 is the Dojo's 30-year anniversary performance. (Courtesy of San Francisco Taiko Dojo.)

The annual community *mochitsuki*, a festival for pounding rice into rice cakes for New Years, takes place in Japantown. (Courtesy of May Murata.)

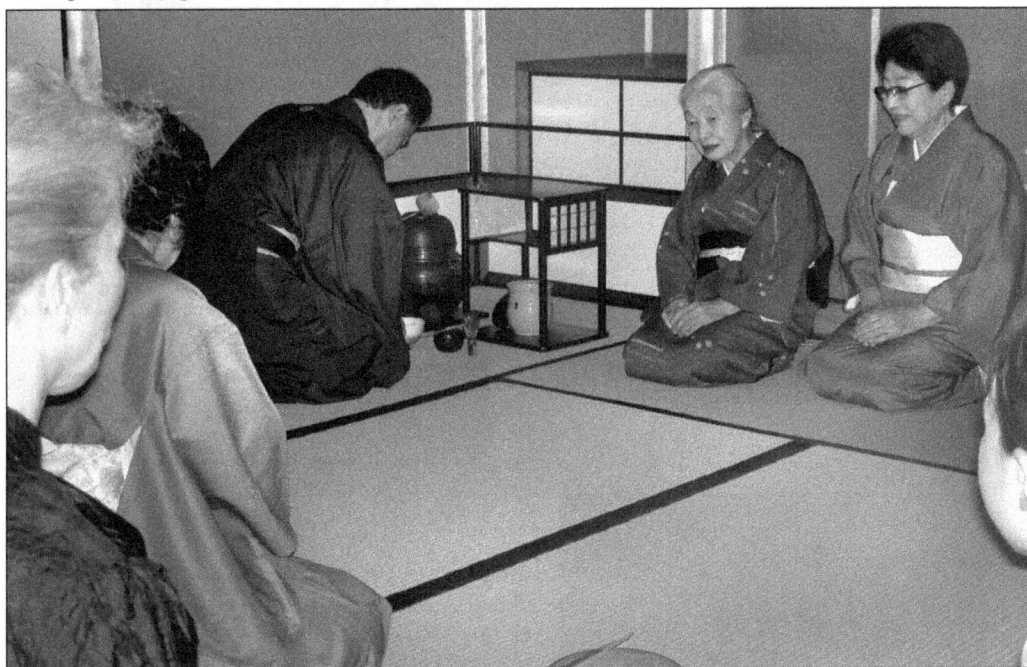

Nichi Bei Kai (Japanese American Association) was officially formed in the late 1800s as a transitional organization for Japanese immigrants adjusting to life in the United States. In 2000, the association merged with the Japanese Speaking Society of America (*Beikoku Nichigo Kyokai*) to form *Hokka Nichi Bei Kai* (Japanese American Association of Northern California). Their building holds a traditional Japanese tea room (*Chashitsu*), donated by the city of Kyoto. (Courtesy of Lucy Kishiue.)

In April 1966, the San Francisco Junior JACL perform their spring show, *Hanasaka Jijii*—a Japanese folk tale. (Courtesy of George Okada.)

In April 1966, the San Francisco Junior JACL Spring Show also included traditional dance by, from left to right, Suzie Kawahata, Georgette Omi, Carol Murata, and Cynthia Hamada. (Courtesy of George Okada.)

The San Francisco chapter of the Japanese American Citizens League participates in numerous community activities including the National AIDS Grove annual workday. Volunteers have helped the grove for over 10 years. This workgroup included members of the Gay Asian Pacific Alliance, chapter member Greg Marutani (fourth from left) and chapter co-president John Handa (fifth from left). (Courtesy of San Francisco JACL/Les Hata.)

Six

PRESERVATION FOR THE GENERATIONS

It is for the contemporary and future generations not to replicate history but to understand their community historically and to use this knowledge in the creation of their own communities in terms of their future contexts. So when we are talking of preservation, it is to preserve not only the icon, but also to preserve the context within which these symbols operated and how they represent the cultural process of community development and to make this information available for the benefit of the community.

—Dr. James Hirabayashi, Ph.D.
Emeritus Professor of Anthropology and Ethnic Studies
San Francisco State University

This 2005 view of *Nihonmachi* today looks west along Post Street. (Courtesy of Misako Mori.)

Buddhist Churh of SF
Buddhist Churh of America headquarters
St. Francis Xavier Catholic Church
(1 block northeast)

Japanese American National Library
Hinode Tower Senior Housing
Kimochi Senior Home

The Sequoias
Senior Apartments

Nihonmachi Terrace
Senior Housing

Kokoro
Senior Assisted
Living Home

Chinese Consulate

Kiss Seafood
Restaurant

to Downtown

LAGUNA STREET

Konkokyo
Church of SF
Konkokyo Church
of North America HQ

Christ United
Presbyterian
Church

Soto Zen Mission
Sokoji Buddhist
Temple

Seiki Plumbing
Kawakami Trading
Futaba Hair Salon
Various Korean American
Businesses

Dentist

New Korea House

Japanese
Garden

EXPRESSWAY

Super 7 Gallery
Watahan Nohara
Import/ Export

Radisson
Miyako Hotel

Korea House

Japanese Community Youth Council
Nichiren Buddhist Church
(1 block north)

Hair & Nail Care

Salon

Union Bank
Hospitality
Room

Beautirun
Beauty Shop

Japantown Task Force
Japanese American Religious Federation
Benevolent Society of California

Nichi Bei Kai
(Japan America Club)
Japanese American
Citizen's League

Uoki K. Sakai
Grocery

Takara
Sushi &
Seafood

Mifune Don
Restaurant

Union Bank
of California

ornamental
bridge

Ornamental
Stone Gallery

Namiki
Apartments

Fujiya Shiseido
Beauty Shop

Seoul
Garden
Restaurant

Ino Sushi
Orange Tree
Boutique

Entry

Genji Antiques

T. Okamoto & Co.
Real Estate, Insurance
Thousand Cranes
Pharmacy

Japanese Video

Super Mira
Market
Yasakuchi
Sweet Shop

Dentists

BJ Creations
Sally's Salon
other offices

Soko Interiors
San Wong Rest.

2nd Floor

Nat'l Japanese American
Historical Society (NJAHS)

Nikkei
Traditions

1st Flogr

Buchanan YMCA

BUCHANAN STREET

Sanko
Art, Ceramics
& Kitchenwares

Bookstore
Offices

JBP Video

Tanpopo Ramen

Iroha &
Shabu-Sen
Restaurants

California Bank
Bank & Trust

Soko Hardware

Umeko
Seafood
Buffet

Kul Shin Bo
Restaurant

Kabuki
Karaoke
Club

BUCHANAN MALL

PEACE PLAZA

GEARY

Cafe
Mums

Benkyo-do
Bakery & Cafe
Paper Tree
Stationery/Origami

Miyako
Restaurant

Peace
Pagoda

Best Western
Miyako Inn

R. Maki Sushi

Kimochi Senior
Center

former
Kokusai
Theater

Sanppo
Sushi Rest.

Kinmon Gakuen School
Nihonmachi
Little Friends

JAM Nihonmachi
Arts Little Friends

Kansai Restaurant

Mizaki, Yuji Law Offices
Aloha Warehouse

Sharaku
Boutique

Dentoh Art
& Crafts

Miseki
Jewelers

Japan
Video

Sakura

Murata's
Cafe Hana
& Florist

Auto
Freak

Japanese Community
& Cultural Center of
Northern California
JCCCNC

Toraya
Apartments

Toraya Restaurant

Daikoku
by Shiki

Isobune
Sushi

Koji
Osakaya
Rest.

May's
Coffee
Shop

Mikado
Gifts

Japanese American
History Archives

Hokubei Mainichi

Radio Mainichi

Mifune
Rest.

Belly
Good

Gifts

Sakura Apartments

Condominiums over
2ndstorefronts
former Japantown Bowl

Kushi
Tsuru
Rest.

Ikenoko
Ikebana

Boutique

The Omadoka
Clothing

WEBSTER STREET

Anderson's
Bakery

Taiyodo
Tea Records

pedestrian bridge

BUSH STREET

Redevelopment Area A-2

SUTTER STREET

POST STREET

Japan Center

KINTETSU MALL

St. Francis Square Cooperative Apartments

Korean Grocery & Doctors Offices

Nihonmachi Apartments

SF Taiko Dojo
Drum/Music Shop
International
Art Guild Galleries
On the Bridge Restaurant

Kimochi Senior Lounge

Asakichi Wares
Asakichi Kimonos
Shige Kimono

SAN FRANCISCO

Japantown

Romen S
Cocktail
Lounge

Sushi
Maki
Rest.

Kinokuniya
Bookstore

Tan Tan
Coffee &
Desserts

Katsura Gardens
Bonsai

1 Hour Japantown
Photo Miniatures

Florist

Kinokuniya
Offices

VAN NESS

MARKET

Negishi
Jewelry Rest.

Boutique
Joy

Sophie's
Crepes

2nd Floor

Suzu Noodle House
(ex Kansseido Manjo)

Aki
Travel

Japan Center
Beauty Clinic

FILLMORE

GEARY

N

Golden Gate
Apartments

Line
Light

Sapporo-ya
Lounge

Mashiko
Folk Craft

Fuku-Sushi

Kinokuniya
Stationery

Izumaya
Rest.

Townhouse
Living Furniture

Mashiko
Folk Craft

Juban Yakiniku
House Restaurant

Asakichi Art Goods

Mon Magazine
Benshi Software

Sanborn map data ©EDR, used by permission.

Redevelopment Area A-2
Redevelopment Area A-1

AMC Kabuki Theater

1st Floor

to Pacific Heights

Toraya Restaurant
& several other shops

Kabuki Hot Springs
(Japanese Baths)

Nichi Bei Times
Newspaper

FILLMORE STREET

to Richmond District
& Cliff House

Fillmore Auditorium

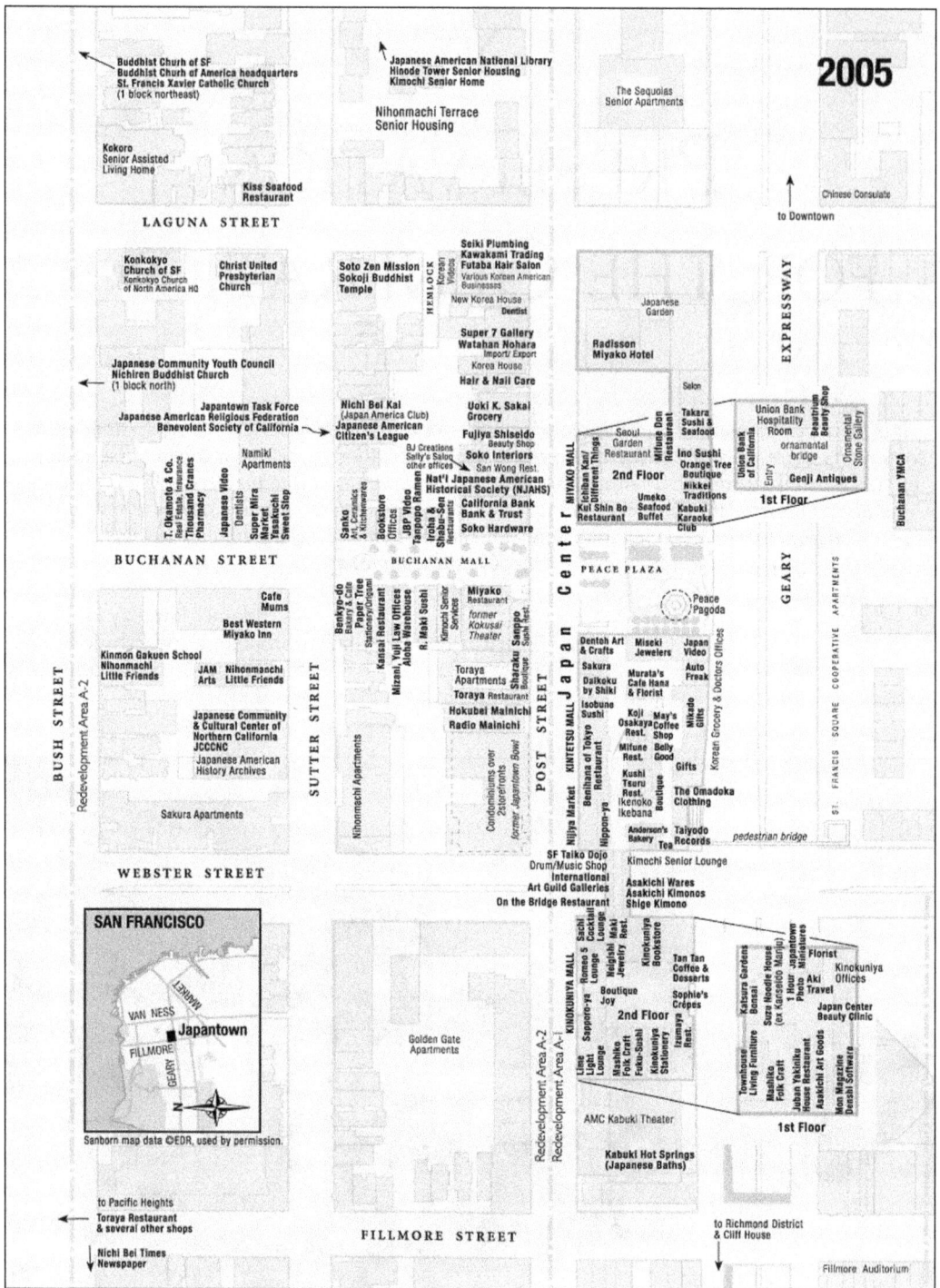

This map shows Japantown and its businesses in 2005. (Courtesy of Ben Pease.)

Anime is a unique style of animation art originating in Japan in the 1950s. Though it has been embraced and copied throughout the world, it remains unique to contemporary Japanese culture. In 1999, while *Sailor Moon* and *Pokemon* were still making their marks on mainstream American television, the first ever Anime Parade was held in San Francisco's Japantown. (Courtesy of Takeshi Onishi/Japan Video.)

With the increasingly popular interest in modified Japanese cars, the Japantown Merchants Association held its first car show in 2000. The show has expanded to over 500 vehicles and the event attracts young people back into Japantown. (Courtesy of Darryl Abantao.)

Children of Nihonmachi Little Friends (NLF) reenact the New Year's tradition of *mochitsuki* (pounding rice) at the annual Oshogatsu Festival. NLF was founded in 1975 by a group of parents, educators, and community-minded activists who were committed to the idea of offering sensitive, bilingual, and low-cost childcare for young children in the community. (Courtesy of Greg Marutani.)

Taking a break at a recent Nihonmachi Street Fair, young taiko students carry on the tradition of community celebration and spirit. (Courtesy of Johnny Nagano.)

Started over 31 years ago by three community activists—Steve Nakajo and Ron and Ken Kanzaki—the Nihonmachi Street Fair is a two-day event that celebrates the cultures of various Asian and Pacific Islander communities around the Bay Area. The event is organized by local youth and allows community-based organizations to raise funds for their respective programs. Live musical performances, exhibits, and food attracts thousands. (Courtesy of Johnny Nagano.)

This multigenerational landmark was dedicated in June 2005 to expresses the past, present, and future of the community through panels representing various stages of Japanese American history, including immigration, wartime incarceration, and perseverance. (Courtesy of Greg Marutani.)

Inscribed on the Japantown landmark is the following poem by San Francisco poet laureate Janice Mirikitani:

I. Sojourners,
Visionaries open hands to the earth,
harvest hope for a future

In America.

II. A journey detained,
interned by injustice,
Manzanar, Tule Lake, Poston, Gila
River, Minidoka, Heart Mountain,
Amache, Topaz, Rohwer, Jerome

What lies before us?

III. Footsteps lead to destiny.
We dance honoring ancestors
who claim our home,
and freedom to pursue our dreams.

Our voices carve a path for justice:
Equal rights for all.

We prevail,
Our future harvested from generations.

From my life
opens countless lives.

The journey continues. . . .